1996

POLITICS IN
CONSTITUTIONAL
LAW

POLITICS IN CONSTITUTIONAL LAW

Cases and Questions

Christopher E. Smith
The University of Akron

Nelson-Hall Publishers/Chicago

Cover Design: Sandi Lawrence
Cover Painting: *Colorforms VI* by Pamela Levin

Library of Congress Cataloging-in-Publication Data

Smith, Christopher E.
    Politics in constitutional law : cases and questions / Christopher
E. Smith.
        p.   cm.
    Includes index.
    ISBN 0-8304-1269-7
    1. United States—Constitutional law—Cases.   2. Political
questions and judicial power—United States—Cases.   3. United
States.   Supreme Court.   I. Title.
KF4549.S55   1992
342.73—dc20
[347.302]   91-33655
                                                      CIP

Manufactured in the United States of America

10   9   8   7   6   5   4   3   2   1

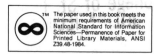

The paper used in this book meets the minimum requirements of American National Standard for Information Sciences—Permanence of Paper for Printed Library Materials, ANSI Z39.48-1984.

For Tim and Jeff

Contents

Preface   ix

1. The Supreme Court and Politics   1
   Suggested Reading

2. Pragmatism and the Structure of Government   9
   Bowsher v. Synar (1986)
   Morrison v. Olson (1988)
   Mistretta v. United States (1989)
   Questions

3. The Justices and the Power of the Judiciary   39
   Mora v. McNamara (1967)
   Holtzman v. Schlesinger (1973)
   Stump v. Sparkman (1978)
   Spallone v. United States (1990)
   Missouri v. Jenkins (1990)
   Questions

4. Judicial Interpretation in Historical Context   65
   Senate Hearings, Public Accommodations (1963)
   Katzenbach v. McClung (1964)
   Daniel v. Paul (1969)
   Questions

5. **The Evolution of Constitutional Interpretation**   79
   Palko v. Connecticut (1937)
   Adamson v. California (1947)
   Rochin v. California (1952)
   Duncan v. Louisiana (1968)
   Questions

6. **The Politics of Capital Punishment**   93
   Enmund v. Florida (1982)
   Tison v. Arizona (1987)
   McCleskey v. Kemp (1987)
   Murray v. Giarratano (1989)
   Butler v. McKellar (1990)
   Questions

7. **The Supreme Court and Political Opposition**   129
   United States v. O'Brien (1968)
   Street v. New York (1969)
   Texas v. Johnson (1989)
   Flag Protection Act of 1989; Legislative History
   United States v. Eichman (1990)
   Questions

8. **Interpersonal Relations and the Tone of Opinions**   155
   Johnson v. Transportation Agency (1987)
   Wards Cove Packing Co. v. Atonio (1989)
   Webster v. Reproductive Health Services (1989)
   County of Allegheny v. A.C.L.U. (1989)
   Holland v. Illinois (1990)
   Questions

   Index of Cases   169

Preface

As a law student, I spent many hours scrutinizing and memorizing Supreme Court cases. In striving to comprehend justices' opinions on a plethora of issues, I neglected to step back from the individual cases in order to question and analyze larger issues affecting the Supreme Court and constitutional law. In retrospect, I recognize how easy it is for students to lose sight of significant issues underlying constitutional law. Students confront a dizzying array of constitutional issues and cases as they attempt to traverse constitutional law's broad terrain within one or two semesters. There are often few opportunities to ponder two of the most important questions that should be addressed to Supreme Court cases: "So what?" and "Why?"

This book provides students with a vehicle for studying and questioning deeply the important influences that affect the development of constitutional law. Whether used alone or in conjunction with a casebook, the book creates opportunities for examination of the Supreme Court's role in the American governing system and the factors that influence justices' decision making.

A major premise underlying the commentaries, cases, and questions presented is that the Supreme Court and constitutional law are best understood as integral components of the American political system. Although the Supreme Court is the quintessential American legal institution with its history, traditions, and authoritative legitimacy, it is intimately connected to the political governing system. In order to understand the reasons that the Supreme Court issues certain decisions and the consequences of those decisions, a student must recognize that the Court is connected to and influenced by "politics."

I am indebted to many people who, whether they realize it or not, contributed to the development of this book. In particular, George Cole and the other faculty members in the Department of Political Science at the University of Connecticut helped me to recognize the linkages between law and politics. My colleagues at the University of Akron provided me with resources and a supportive scholarly environment. Bonnie Ralston and Mari Bell Nolan provided invaluable assistance in the preparation of the manuscript. My wife, Charlotte, my daughter, Alicia, and my son, Eric, were patient and understanding as always.

This book is dedicated to the two people with whom I spent years talking about politics and other issues as my views and ideas developed: my brothers.

ONE

The Supreme Court and Politics

When Americans observe the operation of their governmental institutions, the influence of "politics" is obvious. Political parties compete with each other by making promises to the public in order to gain electoral support for their candidates. Elected officials reward their fellow partisans by appointing them to important positions in government. Public policy decisions by government officials are frequently influenced by the anticipated effects upon a political party's fortunes in upcoming elections. Organized interest groups contribute money for political campaigns in order to gain favors from politicians who are elected to public office.

By contrast, the public has greater expectations for the judiciary. Judges have special training in the law. This specialized knowledge of rules and principles guides judges to seek justice rather than self-interest and political favors. Judges wear black robes and preside over formal proceedings specifically designed to yield fair decisions. In the federal courts, the justices of the Supreme Court, as well as other judges, are insulated from partisan politics through their protected tenure. Thus, these judicial officials apparently follow the neutral principles of law in making decisions rather than succumb to the political influences that affect the other branches of government.

In some respects, these distinctions between the judiciary and other branches of government are correct and meaningful. Judges do have specialized education. In the federal courts, they are insulated from direct involvement in electoral politics. They do follow formal procedures in conducting trials and hearings. These apparent distinctions between the judiciary and other branches of government do not, however, separate courts from "politics." The judiciary is an integral part of the American

1

political system. Moreover, the judges' purported reliance upon "law" in making decisions simply disguises the ways in which the judiciary is inevitably infused with political influences.

Law and Politics

Americans look to the Constitution as the fundamental basis for the United States and its governing system. By extension, the Supreme Court justices, as the ultimate interpreters of the Constitution, possess a special stature as the guardians of national values and social stability under the rule of law. Sanford Levinson, through his "analogy of the Constitution as a sacred text [and] the Supreme Court as a holy institution," describes the way in which the Constitution and constitutional law serve as a "civil religion" that unifies the country.[1] The public's desire to view the Supreme Court and constitutional law as removed from the realm of politics is reinforced by the judiciary's own use of the symbols and imagery of principled neutrality. As Harry Stumpf observes:

> With symbols such as law degrees, robes, walnut-paneled courtrooms, elevated benches, a special language, and the like, we help sustain the myth of an impersonal judiciary divining decisions based on some objective truth contained in the Constitution (another symbol), and knowable only by a select few. It is all a very reassuring view of policy-making (or rather, rule divining), for after the tumult, greed, and indecisiveness of the legislative process—not to mention the excesses, embarrassments and dissonance of the executive policy process—we quickly weary of frustrations and disappointments of plain old POLITICS and wish to repair to the serenity, the sureness, indeed the utter sublimity of JUSTICE, which the LAW and its purveyors promise.[2]

Americans aspire to view courts and law as neutral and principled in order to maintain faith in the righteousness of their governing system. Judges can draw upon this faith to enhance their own legitimacy as authoritative decision makers and to gain acquiescence to their decisions. This belief in the law provides stability for society and vests the judiciary with the authority to participate in processing and resolving divisive societal conflicts.

The image of courts and law does not, however, comport with reality. The judiciary is composed of human beings who, try as they might, can-

1. Sanford Levinson, *Constitutional Faith* (Princeton, NJ: Princeton University Press, 1988), p. 17.
2. Harry P. Stumpf, *American Judicial Politics* (New York: Harcourt Brace Jovanovich, 1988), p. 42.

not escape their "human-ness" in applying their personal attitudes, values, beliefs, and experiences to their judicial decisions. Moreover, the courts are structured and influenced by political forces. Instead of regarding courts and law as separate from politics, it would be more accurate to say, quite simply, "law is politics." Stated more precisely, constitutional law is the product of political processes.

To recognize that judicial institutions and the development of legal doctrine are influenced by political forces does not require that one pessimistically equate judicial processes with the overt manifestations of self-interest and greed contained in partisan politics in the legislative and executive branches. Because of the role and structure of courts, judges do not necessarily possess the same motivations and exhibit the same behaviors as officials in other branches of government. Yet judges' actions, and hence the development of law, are inevitably influenced by political forces.

Although there is no universally accepted definition of "politics," political scientists define "politics" as involving the actors and decision-making processes affecting power, authority, and values in society. Political processes shape government and public policy. The judiciary clearly is involved in the political governing process as well as in the process of allocating and exercising power and authority in society. To say that "law is politics" is merely to recognize that "law" is not what it is often purported to be, namely, a neutral set of consistent principles which can be applied objectively by detached judicial officers. Law is developed and changed by judges—who are public officials selected and influenced by political processes—in order to advance certain values and policies. Thus, courts and law can be best understood by analyzing them as components of the governing political system rather than as unique legal elements that are removed from politics.

The Supreme Court as a Political Institution

There are numerous connections between the Supreme Court and the political system. Because the justices of the Supreme Court bear primary responsibility for the development and articulation of constitutional law, political forces inevitably influence the judicial decisions that determine the evolution of the law.

If constitutional law were based upon consistent, neutral principles, then the law either would not change, or it would evolve gradually. In fact, constitutional law, as defined by the Supreme Court, can change quickly and dramatically. Its development and definition are not dependent upon neutral principles of abstract justice, but rather upon the beliefs and preferences of individual human beings who are placed in positions of authority on the Supreme Court through the operation of political processes. In 1972, for example, the Supreme Court decided that debtors are entitled to a hearing before creditors can seize their property *(Fuentes v. Shevin)*. The Court was split four to three with only seven members participating because recently-appointed Justices Lewis Powell and William Rehnquist had not joined the Court in time to hear oral arguments in the case. Two years later, with the Court at full strength, a new five-member majority, the dissenters from *Fuentes* plus Powell and Rehnquist, produced a contrary result favoring creditors in a case with a similar issue. In dissent, Justice Potter Stewart complained:

> A change in the law upon a ground no firmer than a change in our membership invites the popular misconception that this institution is little different from the two political branches of Government. No misconception could do more lasting injury to this Court and to the system of law which it is our abiding mission to serve.[3]

What Stewart labeled as a "misconception," in fact, reflected reality. The law changed quickly because two new justices, both Republican appointees, disagreed with the justices in the majority in the previous case. The law changed because the political process of appointing new justices created a new mix of philosophies, beliefs, and attitudes among the justices on the Supreme Court. This new development in constitutional law did not flow from neutral principles or eternal truths divined by wise elders on the Court. The decision stemmed from the effects of human, political processes upon the Supreme Court.

The political nature of the Supreme Court can be illustrated in several respects. When it makes decisions about controversial policy issues, the Court must face reactions from other actors and institutions in the political system. These reactions may, in turn, influence the decision making by the Court. The most famous example came during the 1930s when the Supreme Court systematically invalidated state and federal statutes that regulated the economy and advanced social welfare goals. Because the Supreme Court was effectively blocking implementation of the New Deal programs designed to address the economic problems of the Depression era, President Franklin Roosevelt proposed that the size of the Court be changed to permit him to appoint additional justices. Roosevelt's so-called "court packing plan," which would have permitted him to create his own new majority on the Court, caused great political

---

3. Mitchell v. W. T. Grant Company, 416 U.S. 600, 636 (Stewart, J., dissenting), cited in Lucius J. Barker and Twiley W. Barker, *Civil Liberties and the Constitution*, 5th ed. (Englewood Cliffs, NJ: Prentice-Hall, 1986), pp. 541–542.

outcry. It was never passed by Congress, but shortly after it was proposed, the Supreme Court changed its perspective and suddenly began to endorse the economic regulations initiated by Roosevelt. Did justices change their decisions when the structure of the Supreme Court was threatened? No justice would ever admit to such accommodating reactions, but clearly the political environment of that era applied great pressure upon the Court.

Other decisions by the Supreme Court reinforce the notion that justices are cognizant of the political reactions, or potential reactions, to their decisions. In the famous 1954 case of *Brown v. Board of Education*, which finally rejected the official policy of racial segregation in public schools, Chief Justice Earl Warren worked to ensure that the Court would issue a unanimous opinion. He sought unanimity in order to place the full weight of the Court's authority and legitimacy behind the momentous, controversial decision. When the Supreme Court entered the brewing constitutional crisis during Watergate by ordering President Nixon to hand over tape recorded conversations to the special prosecutor, the justices' unanimity apparently deterred Nixon from challenging their authority to issue orders to him *(United States v. Nixon,* 1974).

The Supreme Court does not merely follow the safest political course. It frequently makes unpopular decisions based upon the justices' interpretations of the Constitution and their policy preferences. To say that the justices are influenced by the political environment does not indicate that they lack the will to endure conflicts with other branches of government. The point is merely that the justices' decisions are not based solely upon their theories of law. The justices are also aware that their decisions may cause political upheaval and that they must act prudently to avoid excessive resistance and disobedience.

The composition of the Supreme Court is determined by political processes. Justices have been appointed to the Court for a variety of reasons, but these reasons have always been based upon political considerations rather than upon individual merit. Presidents appoint justices whom they believe will support the values and policies of the president's political party. Presidents select specific appointees in order to gain political approval from ethnic, gender, ideological, or geographical interests. If a president does not like the decisions made by the Supreme Court, then the president can, if given the opportunity, attempt to change those decisions over time by appointing new justices who will lead the evolution of constitutional law in a different direction. President Ronald Reagan significantly altered the composition of the Supreme Court by appointing three new justices and elevating a fourth to chief justice. The Reagan-influenced Court quickly began to change the law by making new decisions affecting racial discrimination, abortion, criminal defendants' rights, and other controversial issues. Because partisan political actors determine the composition of the Supreme Court, the Court's decisions can develop and change in conjunction with changes in national electoral politics.

Within the Supreme Court, the justices can interact strategically with each other in order to advance their legal theories and policy preferences. As Walter Murphy's classic study of the Supreme Court demonstrated, the Court has its own political environment in which justices persuade, bargain, and apply other tactics in order to influence the outcome of cases.[4]

The justices' individual decisions are also tied to politics. Although they claim to follow particular legal theories, it is not difficult to identify instances in which justices deviate from their espoused theories in order to attain specific case outcomes. Moreover, empirical research on justices' decisions shows how specific personal attributes are associated with particular kinds of decisions. For example, justices' political party affiliations and prior experiences as prosecutors are associated with certain kinds of decisions in civil liberties cases.[5] As summarized in an extensive review of the literature on judicial decision making: "[J]udges' decisions are a function of what they prefer to do, tempered by what they think they ought to do, but constrained by what they perceive is feasible to do. Thus, judicial decision making is little different from any other form of decision making."[6] Although justices of the Supreme Court confront difficult questions which are presented in constitutional terms and must be answered in legal language, they still apply their personal attitudes and values in making these important decisions.

The commentaries, cases, and questions in the chapters that follow illuminate the politics involved in the Supreme Court's development of constitutional law. Acknowledgment of the influential role of politics in constitutional law does not entail abandonment of constitutional values. The justices of the Supreme Court generally are, with good faith and the best of intentions, seeking to effectuate the values embodied in the Constitution. The justices, however, do not always agree about precisely which values are contained in the Constitution. As one long-time commentator on the Supreme Court notes:

4. Walter F. Murphy, *Elements of Judicial Strategy* (Chicago: University of Chicago Press, 1964).

5. C. Neal Tate, "Personal Attribute Models of the Voting Behavior of U.S. Supreme Court Justices: Liberalism in Civil Liberties and Economics Decisions, 1946–1978," *American Political Science Review* (1981) 75:355–367.

6. James L. Gibson, "From Simplicity to Complexity: The Development of Theory in the Study of Judicial Behavior," *Political Behavior* (1983) 5: 9.

The justices' constitutional interpretations owe more to political ideologies than they pretend. But far more than Congress, far more than any recent president, justices reach decisions by searching their consciences, carefully sifting facts and law, trying to do right as they see the right.[7]

The justices cannot, however, identify and advance constitutional values through a neutral, idealized legal process removed from politics. As human beings who are both products of and attached to the political system, the justices invariably shape their decisions in accordance with a variety of political influences. Although it is important to study Supreme Court opinions containing the legal theories and justifications for the justices' decisions, the development of constitutional law cannot be understood without examining the political influences and consequences that underlie Supreme Court cases.

Suggested Reading

Abraham, Henry J. *Justices and Presidents: A Political History of Appointments to the Supreme Court,* 2nd ed. New York; Oxford University Press, 1985.

A detailed examination of the appointment of justices to the Supreme Court, including discussion of their backgrounds and the political factors underlying their nominations.

Goldman, Sheldon, and Thomas J. Jahnige. *The Federal Courts as a Political System,* 3rd ed. New York: Harper and Row, 1985.

Presents a useful model for conceptualizing the courts as integral components within the political system which interact with and respond to other political actors and institutions.

Irons, Peter. *The Courage of Their Convictions.* New York: Free Press, 1988.

The personal stories of individuals who brought controversial cases before the Supreme Court, including discussion of the political environment in which the Court responded to those cases.

Murphy, Walter F. *Elements of Judicial Strategy.* Chicago: University of Chicago Press, 1964.

---

7. Stuart Taylor, Jr., "Season of Snarling Justices," *Akron Beacon Journal,* April 5, 1990, p. A11.

A study of the strategies and tactics employed by justices within the Supreme Court in attempting to persuade or induce their colleagues to join their opinions.

O'Brien, David M. *Storm Center: The Supreme Court in American Politics*, 2nd ed. New York: W. W. Norton, 1990.

A thorough account of the Supreme Court's history and decision-making processes.

Wasby, Stephen L. *The Supreme Court in the Federal Judicial System*, 3rd ed. Chicago: Nelson-Hall, 1988.

A comprehensive examination of the Supreme Court's decision-making process and role in the American political system, including extensive coverage of academic studies of the Court.

Woodward, Bob, and Scott Armstrong. *The Brethren: Inside the Supreme Court*, New York: Simon and Schuster, 1979.

Although its factual accuracy has been challenged, this is an engrossing journalistic account of the personalities, relationships, and tactics of the justices during the early 1970s.

TWO

Pragmatism and the Structure of Government

The Constitution of the United States divides the federal government into three branches. Article I of the Constitution describes the structure and powers of the legislative branch. Articles II and III serve the same purposes for the executive and judicial branches respectively. This division of power within the structure of government was designed as a protection against the accumulation of excessive power within a single institution. As James Madison declared in Federalist No. 47: "The accumulation of all powers, legislative, executive, and judiciary, in the same hands, ... may justly be pronounced the very definition of tyranny."

The Constitution further diminishes this risk of "tyranny" not only by dividing power within government, but also by granting the various branches "checks and balances" over the actions of other governmental institutions. For example, the president can veto legislation by Congress and the Senate must approve presidential appointments to the Supreme Court and other high offices. The system of checks and balances ensures that separation of powers does not become complete. The functions of government are blended together. For example, both Congress and the president participate in the legislative process, and both the executive and legislative branches monitor the activities of executive agencies. As Chief Justice Warren Burger declared in *United States v. Nixon* (1974):

> In designing the structure of our Government and dividing and allocating the sovereign power among three coequal branches, the Framers of the Constitution sought to provide a comprehensive system, but the separate powers were not intended to operate with absolute independence.

9

This fusing of governmental powers complicates the task of allocating authority among the branches.

Although the Constitution provides the fundamental basis for the structure of American government, it does not clearly answer all questions that may arise about the distribution of power. In one sense, this would appear to be a significant weakness in the Constitution. If conflicts develop over the appropriate distribution of authority and the Constitution does not provide a clear answer, how will the matter be resolved? On the other hand, Archibald Cox argues that the Constitution's greatest strength is that it leaves the precise details of the governing system to be worked out by the people as the country evolves and social conditions change:

> In retrospect we can see that much of the genius of the Founding Fathers, perhaps forced upon them by their very differences, lay in their remarkable capacity for saying enough but not too much—just enough to give those who would come after them a point of reference and a strong foundation on which to build, but not so much as to inhibit their successors, who would live in changed and changing worlds.[1]

The ambiguity within the Constitution inevitably left certain aspects of the government structure open for evolutionary development. As Louis Fisher notes, "[t]he boundaries between the three branches of government are . . . strongly affected by custom and acquiescence."[2] For example, the judiciary did not gain any explicit check over the other branches from the words of the Constitution. The Supreme Court, however, initiated its own substantial power to examine the constitutional validity of acts by the president and Congress, namely the power of "judicial review," in the famous case of *Marbury v. Madison* (1803). Although this power was rarely exercised until after the Civil War, judicial review became accepted as a component of the governing structure as it was applied with increasing frequency—despite the fact that it is not mentioned in the Constitution. In essence, any gaps in the Constitution's allocation of power are filled by branches which assert new authority and then wait to see whether the other branches will challenge or accept this new distribution of governmental power.

If there is a challenge to a branch's assertion of power, who will decide what is permissible under the Constitution? The Supreme Court

---

1. Archibald Cox, *The Supreme Court and the Constitution* (Boston, MA: Houghton Mifflin, 1987), p. 42.
2. Louis Fisher, *American Constitutional Law* (New York: McGraw-Hill, 1990), p. 217.

bears that responsibility. Although the judiciary can be one of the contending parties in these conflicts over the allocation of power, the courts have, thus far, been accepted as the umpires of these disputes. This acceptance is determined not by any inherent formal power possessed by the judiciary to work its will over the other branches of government, but instead depends upon the perceived legitimacy of judicial opinions. If the Court's actions are regarded as legitimate, they will consequently generate support and acceptance from other political forces within the country. The dispute over President Nixon's Watergate tapes provides a good example of this process through which power assertion, conflict, political reactions, and acquiescence determine the allocation and definition of governmental power.

In 1974, when President Nixon refused to turn over tape recordings of conversations within the White House which the Special Prosecutor believed would provide evidence in the investigation of Watergate-related criminal activities, Nixon claimed that his "executive privilege" as president prevented anyone from ordering him to hand over the tapes. His assertion was based on the premise that the executive branch has certain powers over its own internal documents and deliberations which are immune from interference by the other branches of government. When the Supreme Court declared that a criminal investigation takes precedence over claims of "executive privilege" (*United States v. Nixon*, 1974), the country waited to see whether Nixon would obey the Supreme Court. Because the Court was unanimous and thereby vested its full authority and legitimacy in the decision, Nixon acquiesced. The Supreme Court had no power to force Nixon physically to relinquish the tapes. It could not arrest him or fine him or seize the tapes. The real pressure on the president came from Congress and public opinion which would push forward with the impeachment process if Nixon ignored a unanimous Supreme Court decision. The conflicting assertions of authority between the executive and judicial branches were resolved by the reactions or potential reactions of the other dominant political forces in the country, namely the legislative branch and the public. Because the other political forces in society supported the legitimacy of the unanimous Supreme Court decision, Nixon backed down and acquiesced to a new precedent defining the scope of the president's "executive privilege" authority.

The *Nixon* case represented a significant constitutional crisis in which the future of the country's governing system hinged upon the resolution of a dispute between the president and other political actors. Other conflicts over the separation of powers in government are less monumental. Frequently, the public has little interest in the disputes between government institutions over authority to make specific decisions.

In these instances, a branch of government, usually Congress or the president, may attempt to resolve a perceived problem in the structure of government by initiating an innovative action and then hoping for acquiescence by the other branches. If a contending branch challenges the new assertion of authority, the courts must determine the proper allocation of power under the Constitution.

All of the relevant actors within the political system are keenly aware that the purpose of the separation of powers principle is to prevent the accumulation of excessive power within one branch of government. They do not necessarily agree, however, on the definition of circumstances in which the principle is violated. When is an accumulation of power "excessive"? When do problems facing the government require adjustments or innovations in the definition and allocation of power for the various branches? These questions are not easily answered because the Constitution does not explicitly discuss or even anticipate the kinds of conflicts that may arise among the branches of government, especially as the federal government has become larger and more complex over the course of two centuries.

When facing these separation of powers issues, the justices of the Supreme Court are frequently confronted with a fundamental choice: adherence to a rigid theory of relatively clearly separated powers or pragmatic acceptance of innovations which, despite blurring the lines of authority, address a difficult problem facing the government. In the 1980s, the Supreme Court's approach to evaluating innovative actions by Congress appeared to change from a rigid conception of separation of powers, which operated to strike down innovative Congressional actions, to a more pragmatic acceptance of new initiatives designed to address specific goals and problems facing the government. In 1983, the Supreme Court struck down the legislative veto process utilized by Congress (*Immigration and Naturalization Service v. Chadha*). The Supreme Court felt that the legislative branch improperly infringed upon presidential authority by delegating to the executive branch decision-making authority about the details of specific programs, but reserving for itself the authority to veto executive decisions through the actions of the individual houses of Congress. In dissent, Justice Byron White pragmatically called the legislative veto "the central means by which Congress secures the accountability of executive and independent agencies." Although the majority opinion "concede[d] this utilitarian argument," Chief Justice Burger insisted that "the powers delegated to the three Branches are functionally identifiable." Burger and the other justices in the majority declared that the legislative and executive functions must be separated in this case even if they "impose burdens on governmental processes that often seem clumsy, inefficient, [and] even unworkable."

In the cases that follow, the Supreme Court first maintains a rigid conception of separation of powers (*Bowsher v. Synar*, 1986), but subsequently takes a more pragmatic approach to innovations addressing specific governmental problems (*Morrison v. Olson*, 1988; *Mistretta v. United States*, 1989). These decisions not only affect how the government operates but also raise questions about why the Supreme Court changes its approach to the interpretation of the Constitution.

BOWSHER v. SYNAR

478 U.S. 714 (1986)

Chief Justice BURGER delivered the opinion of the Court [joined by Justices BRENNAN, POWELL, REHNQUIST, and O'CONNOR]:

The question presented by these appeals is whether the assignment by Congress to the Comptroller General of the United States of certain functions under the Balanced Budget and Emergency Deficit Control Act of 1985 violates the doctrine of separation of powers.

I

A

On December 12, 1985, the President signed into law the Balanced Budget and Emergency Deficit Control Act of 1985 . . . , popularly known as the "Gramm-Rudman-Hollings Act." The purpose of the Act is to eliminate the federal budget deficit. To that end, the Act sets a "maximum deficit amount" for federal spending for each of fiscal years 1986 through 1991. The size of that maximum deficit amount progressively reduces to zero in fiscal year 1991. If in any fiscal year the federal budget deficit exceeds the maximum deficit amount by more than a specified sum, the Act requires across-the-board cuts in federal spending to reach the targeted deficit level, with half of the cuts made to defense programs and the other half made to non-defense programs. The Act exempts certain priority programs from these cuts. . . .

These "automatic" reductions are accomplished through a rather complicated procedure . . . , the so-called "reporting provisions" of the Act. Each year, the Directors of the Office of Management and Budget (OMB) and the Congressional Budget Office (CBO) independently estimate the amount of the federal budget deficit for the upcoming fiscal year. If that deficit exceeds the maximum targeted deficit amount for that fiscal year by more than a specified amount, the Directors of OMB and CBO independently calculate, on a program-by-program basis, the budget reductions necessary to ensure that the deficit does not exceed the maximum deficit amount. The Act then requires the Directors to report jointly their deficit estimates and budget reduction calculations to the Comptroller General.

The Comptroller General, after reviewing the Directors' reports, then reports his conclusions to the President. . . . The President in turn must issue a "sequestration" order mandating the spending reductions specified by the Comptroller General. . . . There follows a period during which Congress may by legislation reduce spending to obviate, in whole or in part, the need for the sequestration order. If such reductions are not enacted, the sequestration order becomes effective and the spending reductions included in that order are made.

Anticipating constitutional challenge to these procedures, the Act also contains a "fallback" deficit reduction process to take effect "[i]n the event that any of the reporting procedures . . . are invalidated.". . . . Under these provisions, the report prepared by the Directors of OMB and CBO is submitted directly to a specially-created Temporary Joint Committee on Deficit Reduction, which must report in five days to both Houses a joint resolution setting forth the content of the Directors' report. Congress then must vote on the resolution under special rules, which render amendments out of order. If the resolution is passed and signed by the President, it then serves as the basis for a Presidential sequestration order.

B

Within hours of the President's signing of the Act, Congressman Synar, who had voted against the Act, filed a complaint seeking declaratory relief that the Act was unconstitutional. Eleven other Members later joined Congressman Synar's suit. A virtually identical lawsuit was also filed by the National Treasury Employees Union. The Union alleged that its members had been injured as a result of the Act's automatic spending reduction provisions, which have suspended certain cost-of-living benefit increases to the Union's members.

A three-judge District Court . . . invalidated the reporting provisions. *Synar v. United States*, 626 F.Supp. 1374 (D.C. 1986) (Scalia, Johnson, Gasch, JJ.). . . .

[T]he District Court . . . held that the role of the Comptroller General in the deficit reduction process violated the constitutionally imposed separation of powers. The court first explained that the Comptroller General exercises executive functions under the Act. However, the Comptroller General, while appointed by the President with the advice and consent of the Senate, is removable not by the President but only by a joint resolution of Congress or by impeachment. The District Court reasoned that this arrangement could not be sustained under this Court's decisions in *Myers v. United States*, 272 U.S. 52 . . . (1926), and *Humphrey's Executor v. United States*, 295 U.S. 602 . . . (1935). Under the separation of powers established by the Framers of the Constitution, the court concluded, Congress may not retain the power of removal over an officer performing executive functions. The congressional removal power created a "here-and-now subservience" of the Comptroller General to Congress. . . . The District Court therefore held that

> "since the powers conferred upon the Comptroller General as part of the automatic deficit reduction process are executive powers, which cannot constitutionally be exercised by an officer removable by Congress, those powers cannot be exercised and therefore the automatic deficit reduction process to which they are central cannot be implemented". . . .

Appeals were taken directly to this Court pursuant to . . . the Act. . . .

III

We noted recently that "[t]he Constitution sought to divide the delegated powers of the new Federal Government into three defined categories, Legislative, Executive, and Judicial." *INS v. Chadha*, 462 U.S. 919, 951 . . . (1983). The declared purpose of separating and dividing the powers of government, of course, was to diffus[e] power the better to secure liberty." *Youngstown Sheet & Tube Co. v. Sawyer*, 343 U.S. 579, 635 . . . (1952) (Jackson, J., concurring). Justice Jackson's words echo the famous warning of Montesquieu, quoted by James Madison in The Federalist No. 47, that " 'there can be no liberty where the legislative and executive powers are united in the same person, or body of magistrates'". . . .

Even a cursory examination of the Constitution reveals the influence of Montesquieu's thesis that checks and balances were the foundation of the structure of government that would protect liberty. The Framers provided a vigorous legislative branch and a separate and wholly independent executive branch, with each branch responsible ultimately to the people. . . .

That this system of division and separation of powers produces conflicts, confusion, and discordance at times is inherent, but it was deliberately so structured to assure full, vigorous and open debate on the great issues affecting the people and to provide avenues for the operation of checks on the exercise of governmental power.

The Constitution does not contemplate an active role for Congress in the supervision of officers charged with the execution of the laws it enacts. The President appoints "Officers of the United States" with the "Advice and Consent of the Senate . . . ." Article II, [section] 2. Once the appointment has been made and confirmed, however, the Constitution explicitly provides for removal of Officers of the United States by Congress only upon impeachment by the House of Representatives and conviction by the Senate. An impeachment by the House and trial by the Senate can rest only on "Treason, Bribery or other high Crimes and Misdemeanors." Article II, [section] 4. A direct congressional role in the removal of officers charged with the execution of the laws beyond this limited one is inconsistent with separation of powers.

This was made clear in debate in the First Congress in 1789. . . .

This Court first directly addressed this issue in *Myers v. United States* . . . (1925). At issue in *Myers* was a statute providing that certain postmasters could be removed only "by and with the advice and consent of the Senate." The President removed one such postmaster without Senate approval, and a lawsuit ensued. Chief Justice Taft, writing for the Court, declared the statute unconstitutional on the ground that for Congress to "draw to itself, or to either branch of it, the power to remove or the right to participate in the exercise of that power . . . would be . . . to infringe the constitutional principle of the separation of governmental powers.". . .

A decade later, . . . *Humphrey's Executor* involved an issue not presented either in the *Myers* case or in this case—*i.e.* the power of Congress to limit the President's powers of removal of a Federal Trade Commissioner. . . . The relevant statute permitted removal "by the President," but only "for inefficiency, neglect of duty, or malfeasance in office." Justice Sutherland, speaking for the Court, upheld the statute, holding that "illimitable power of removal is not possessed by the President [with respect to Federal Trade Commissioners]." . . . The Court distinguished *Myers*, reaffirming its holding that congressional participation in the removal of executive officers is unconstitutional. . . .

In light of these precedents, we conclude that Congress cannot reserve for itself the power of removal of an officer charged with the execution of laws except by impeachment. To permit the execution of the laws to be vested in an officer answerable only to Congress would, in practical terms, reserve in Congress control over the execution of the laws . . . The structure of the Constitution does not permit Congress to execute the laws; it follows that Congress cannot grant to an officer under its control what it does not possess.

Our decision in *INS v. Chadha* 462 U.S. 919 . . . (1983), supports this conclusion. . . . To permit an officer controlled by Congress to execute the laws would be, in essence, to permit a congressional veto. Congress could simply remove, or threaten to remove, an officer for executing the laws in any fashion found to be unsatisfactory to Congress. This kind of congressional control over the execution of the laws, *Chadha* makes clear, is constitutionally impermissible. . . .

IV

Appellants urge that the Comptroller General performs his duties independently and is not subservient to Congress. We agree with the District Court that this contention does not bear close scrutiny.

The critical factor lies in the provisions of the statute defining the Comptroller General's office relating to removability. Although the Comptroller General is nominated by the president from a list of three individuals recommended by the Speaker of the House of Representatives and the President pro tempore of the Senate, . . . and confirmed by the Senate, he is removable only at the initiative of Congress. He may be removed not only by impeachment but also by Joint Resolution of Congress "at any time" resting on any one of the following bases:

> "(i) permanent disability;
> "(ii) inefficiency;
> "(iii) neglect of duty;
> "(iv) malfeasance; or
> "(v) a felony or conduct involving moral turpitude."
> 31 U.S.C. [section] 703(e)(1). . . .

[T]he dissent's assessment of the statute fails to recognize the breadth of the grounds for removal. The statute permits removal for "inefficiency," "neglect of duty," or "malfeasance." These terms are very broad and, as interpreted by Congress, could sustain removal of a Comptroller General for any number of actual or perceived transgressions of the legislative will. The Constitutional Convention chose to permit impeachment of executive officers only for "Treason, Bribery, or other high Crimes and Misdemeanors." It rejected language that would have permitted impeachment for "maladministration," with Madison arguing that "[s]o vague a term will be equivalent to a tenure during pleasure of the Senate.". . .

Justice WHITE, however, assures us that "[r]ealistic consideration" of the "practical result of the removal provision," . . . reveals that the Comptroller General is unlikely to be removed by Congress. The separated powers of our government can not be permitted to turn on judicial assessment of whether an officer exercising executive power is on good terms with Congress. The Framers recognized that, in the long term, structural protections against abuse of power were critical to preserving liberty. In constitutional terms, the removal powers over the Comptroller General's office dictate that he will be subservient to Congress. . . .

It is clear that Congress has consistently viewed the Comptroller General as an officer of the Legislative Branch. . . .

Over the years, the Comptrollers General have also viewed themselves as part of the Legislative Branch. . . .

Against this backdrop, we see no escape from the conclusion that, because Congress had retained removal authority over the Comptroller General, he may not be entrusted with executive powers. The remaining question is whether the Comptroller General has been assigned such powers in the Balanced Budget and Emergency Deficit Control Act of 1985.

V

The primary responsibility of the Comptroller General under the instant Act is the preparation of a "report." This report must contain detailed estimates of projected federal revenues and expenditures. The report must also specify the reductions, if any, necessary to reduce the deficit to the target for the appropriate fiscal year. The reductions must be set forth on a program-by-program basis. . . .

Appellants suggest that the duties assigned to the Comptroller General in the Act are essentially ministerial and mechanical so that their performance does not constitute "execution of the law" in a meaningful sense. On the contrary, we view these functions as plainly entailing execution of the law in constitutional terms. Interpreting a law enacted by Congress to implement the legislative mandate is the very essence of "execution" of the law. Under [section] 251, the Comptroller General must exercise judgment concerning facts that affect the application of the Act. He must also interpret the provisions of the Act to determine precisely what budgetary calculations are required. Decisions of that kind are typically made by officers charged with executing a statute. . . .

Congress of course initially determined the content of the Balanced Budget and Emergency Deficit Control Act; and undoubtedly the content of the Act determines the nature of the executive duty. However, as *Chadha* makes clear, once Congress makes its choice in enacting legislation, its participation ends. Congress can thereafter control the execution of its enactment only indirectly—by passing new legislation. . . . By placing the responsibility for the execution of the Balanced Budget and Emergency Deficit Control Act in the hands of an officer who is subject to removal only by itself, Congress in effect has retained control over the execution of the Act and has intruded into the executive function. The Constitution does not permit such an intrusion. . . .

VII

No one can doubt that Congress and the President are confronted with fiscal and economic problems of unprecedented magnitude, but "the fact that a given law or procedure is efficient, convenient, and useful in facilitating functions of government, standing alone, will not save it if it is contrary to the Constitution. Convenience and efficiency are not the primary objectives—or the hallmarks—of democratic government. . . ." *Chadha* . . . at 944. . . .

[Justice STEVENS, joined by Justice MARSHALL, concurred in the judgment, but argued that Congress may not authorize a representative, such as the Comptroller General, to act on its behalf. Instead, all actions by Congress, including specific deficit reduction decisions, must be passed by both houses of Congress and presented to the President for signature or veto.]

Justice WHITE, dissenting:

The Court, acting in the name of separation of powers, takes upon itself to strike down the Gramm-Rudman-Hollings Act, one of the most novel and far-reaching legislative responses to a national crisis since the New Deal. The basis of the Court's action is a solitary provision of another statute [regarding removal of the Comptroller General] that was passed over sixty years ago and has lain dormant since that time. . . . [I question] the wisdom of the Court's willingness to interpose its distressingly formalistic views of separation of powers as a bar to the attainment of governmental objectives through the means chosen by the Congress and the President in the legislative process established by the Constitution. . . . [T]he Court's decision rests on a feature of the legislative scheme that is of minimal practical significance and that presents no substantial threat to the basic scheme of separation of powers. . . .

[T]he substantial role played by the President in the process of removal through joint resolution reduces to utter insignificance the possibility that the threat of removal will induce subservience to the Congress. As I have pointed out above, a joint resolution must be presented to the President and is ineffective if it is vetoed by him, unless the veto is overridden by the constitutionally prescribed two-thirds majority of both Houses of Congress. The requirement of presidential approval obviates the possibility that the Comptroller will perceive himself so completely at the mercy of Congress that he will function as its tool. If the Comptroller's conduct in office is not so unsatisfactory to the President as to convince the latter that removal is required under the statutory standard, Congress will have no independent power to coerce the Comptroller unless it can muster a two-thirds majority in both Houses—a feat of bipartisanship more difficult than that required to impeach and convict. . . .

The practical result of the removal provision is not to render the Comptroller unduly dependent upon or subservient to Congress, but to render him one of the most independent officers in the entire federal establishment. . . .

Realistic consideration of the nature of the Comptroller General's relation to Congress thus reveals that the threat to separation of powers conjured up by the majority is wholly chimerical. . . .

The majority's . . . conclusion rests on rigid dogma. . . . Reliance on such an unyielding principle to strike down a statute posing no real danger of aggrandizement of congressional power is extremely misguided and insensitive to our constitutional role. . . .

Justice BLACKMUN, dissenting:

. . . . The only relief sought in this case is nullification of the automatic budget-reduction provisions of the Deficit Control Act, and that relief should not be awarded even if the Court is correct that those provisions are constitutionally incompatible with Congress' authority to remove the Comptroller General by joint resolution. Any incompatibility, I feel, should be cured by refusing to allow congressional removal—if it ever is attempted—and not by striking down the central provisions of the Deficit Control Act. However wise or foolish it may be, that statute unquestionably ranks among the most important federal enactments of the past several decades. I cannot see the sense of invalidating legislation of this magnitude in order to preserve a cumbersome, 65-year-old removal power that has never been exercised and appears to have been all but forgotten until this litigation.

I

. . . .

Under the District Court's approach, everything depends on who first files suit. Because Representative Synar and the plaintiffs who later joined him in this case objected to budget cuts made pursuant to the Deficit Control Act, the District Court struck down that statute. But if the Comptroller General had filed suit 15 minutes before the Congressman did, seeking a declaratory judgment that the 1921 removal power could not constitutionally be exercised in light of the duties delegated to the Comptroller General in 1985 [under the Deficit Control Act], the removal provision presumably would have been invalidated, and the Deficit Control Act would have survived intact. Momentous issues of public law should not be decided in so arbitrary a fashion. In my view, the only sensible way to choose between the two conjunctively unconstitutional statutory provisions is to determine which provision can be invalidated with the least disruption of congressional motives. . . .

II

. . . .

In the absence of express statutory direction, I think it is plain that, as both Houses urge, invalidating the Comptroller General's functions under the Deficit Control Act would frustrate congressional objectives far more seriously than would refusing to allow Congress to exercise its removal authority [over the Comptroller General] under the 1921 law. . . .

MORRISON v. OLSON

108 S. Ct. 2597 (1988)

Chief Justice REHNQUIST delivered the opinion of the Court [joined by Justices BLACKMUN, BRENNAN, MARSHALL, O'CONNOR, STEVENS, and WHITE. Justice KENNEDY did not participate in the decision]:

This case presents us with a challenge to the independent counsel provisions of the Ethics in Government Act of 1978. . . . We hold today that these provisions of the Act do not violate the Appointments Clause of the Constitution, . . . or the limitations of Article III, nor do they impermissibly interfere with the President's authority under Article II in violation of the constitutional principle of separation of powers.

I

Briefly stated, Title VI of the Ethics in Government Act . . . , allows for the appointment of an "independent counsel" to investigate and, if appropriate, prosecute certain high ranking government officials for violations of federal criminal laws. The Act requires the Attorney General, upon receipt of information that he determines is "sufficient to constitute grounds to investigate whether any person [covered under the Act] may have violated any Federal criminal law," to conduct a preliminary investigation of the matter. When the Attorney General has completed this investigation, or 90 days has elapsed, he is required to report to a special court (the Special Division) created by the Act "for the purpose of appointing independent counsels." . . . If, however, the Attorney General has determined that there are "reasonable grounds to believe that further investigation or prosecution is warranted," then he "shall apply to the division of the court for the appointment of an independent counsel." . . . Upon receiving this application, the Special Division "shall appoint an appropriate independent counsel and shall define that independent counsel's prosecutorial jurisdiction. . . ."

Two statutory provisions govern the length of an independent counsel's tenure in office. The first defines the procedure for removing an independent counsel. . . . :

> "An independent counsel appointed under this chapter may be removed from office, other than by impeachment and conviction, only by the personal action of the Attorney General and only for good cause, physical disability, mental incapacity, or any other condition that substantially impairs the performance of such independent counsel's duties."

If an independent counsel is removed pursuant to this section, the Attorney General is required to submit a report to both the Special Division and the Judiciary Committees of the Senate and House "specifying the facts found and the ultimate grounds for such removal. . . ."

The other provision governing the tenure of the independent counsel defines the procedures for "terminating" the counsel's office. Under [section] 596(b)(1), the office of an independent counsel terminates when he notifies the Attorney General that he has completed or substantially completed any investigations or prosecutions undertaken pursuant to the Act. In addition, the Special Division, acting either on its own or on the suggestion of the Attorney General, may terminate the office of an independent counsel at any time if it finds that "the investigation of all matters . . . have been completed or so substantially completed that it would be appropriate for the Department of Justice to complete such investigations and prosecutions". . . .

III

. . . The parties do not dispute that "[t]he Constitution for purposes of appointment . . . divides all its officers into two classes." *United States v. Germaine* . . . (1879). As we stated in *Buckley v. Valeo* . . . (1976), "[p]rincipal officers are selected by the President with the advice and consent of the Senate. Inferior officers Congress may allow to be appointed by the President alone, by the heads of departments, or by the Judiciary." The initial question is, accordingly, whether [the independent counsel] is an "inferior" or a "principal" officer. If she is the latter, as the Court of Appeals concluded, then the Act is in violation of the Appointments Clause [of the Constitution requiring presidential appointment and Senate confirmation].

The line between "inferior" and "principal" officers is one that is far from clear, and the Framers provided little guidance into where it should be drawn. . . . [I]n our view [the independent counsel] clearly falls on the "inferior officer" side of that line. Several factors lead to this conclusion.

First, [the independent counsel] is subject to removal by a higher Executive Branch official . . . Second, [the independent counsel] is empowered by the Act to perform only certain, limited duties. . . .

Third, [the independent counsel's] office is limited in jurisdiction. . . . [A]n independent counsel can only act within the scope of the jurisdiction that has been granted by the Special Division pursuant to a request by the Attorney General. Finally, [the independent counsel's] office is limited in tenure. . . . In our view, these factors relating to the "ideas of tenure, duration . . . and duties" of the independent counsel . . . are sufficient to establish that appellant is an "inferior" officer in the constitutional sense. . . .

IV

. . . We have long recognized that by the express provision of Article III, the judicial power of the United States is limited to "Cases" and "Controversies." . . . As a general rule, we have broadly stated that "executive or administrative duties of a nonjudicial nature may not be imposed on judges holding office under Article III of the Constitution." . . . The purpose of this limitation is to help ensure the independence of the Judicial Branch and to prevent the judiciary from encroaching into areas reserved for the other branches. . . .

[T]he Act vests in the [judges of] the Special Division the power to choose who will serve as independent counsel and the power to define his or her jurisdiction. . . . In our view, Congress' power under the [Appointments] Clause to vest "Appointment" of inferior officers in the courts may, in certain circumstances, allow Congress to give the courts some discretion in defining the nature and scope of the appointed official's authority. . . .

[T]he Special Division's power to terminate the office of independent counsel . . . is not a power that could be considered typically "judicial," as it has few analogues among the court's more traditional powers. Nonetheless, we do not, as did the Court of Appeals, view this provision as a significant judicial encroachment upon executive power or upon the prosecutorial discretion of the independent counsel. . . .

. . . [The Special Division's termination power] is basically a device for removing from the public payroll an independent counsel who has served her purpose, but is unwilling to acknowledge the fact. So construed, the Special Division's power to terminate does not pose a sufficient threat of judicial intrusion into matters that are more properly within the Executive's authority to require that the Act be invalidated as inconsistent with Article III. . . .

V

We now turn to consider whether the Act is invalid under the constitutional principle of separation of powers. Two related issues must be addressed: the first is whether the provision of the Act restricting the Attorney General's power to remove the independent counsel to only those instances in which he can show "good cause," taken by itself, impermissibly interferes with the President's exercise of his constitutionally appointed functions. The second is whether, taken as a whole, the Act violates the separation of powers by reducing the President's ability to control the prosecutorial powers wielded by the independent counsel.

A

. . . .

Unlike both *Bowsher* and *Myers*, this case does not involve an attempt by Congress itself to gain a role in the removal of executive officials other than its established powers of impeachment and conviction. The Act instead puts the removal power squarely in the hands of the Executive Branch [by permitting removal by the Attorney General for "good cause"]. . . . [T]he removal provisions of the Act make this case more analogous to *Humphrey's Executor* . . . than to *Myers* or *Bowsher*. . . .

. . . The real question is whether the removal restrictions are of such a nature that they impede the President's ability to perform his constitutional duty, and the functions of the officials in question must be analyzed in that light.

Considering for the moment the "good cause" removal provision in isolation from the other parts of the Act at issue in this case, we cannot say that the imposition of a "good cause" standard for removal by itself unduly trammels on executive authority. . . . Although the [independent] counsel exercises no small amount of discretion and judgment in deciding how to carry out her duties under the Act , we simply do not see how the President's need to control the exercise of that discretion is so central to the functioning of the Executive Branch as to require as a matter of constitutional law that the counsel be terminable at will by the President. . . .

B

The final question to be addressed is whether the Act, taken as a whole, violates the principle of separation of powers by unduly interfering with the role of the Executive Branch. Time and again we have reaffirmed the importance in our constitutional scheme of the separation of governmental powers into the three coordinate branches. . . . On the other hand, we have never held that the Constitution requires that the three branches of Government "operate with absolute independence." . . .

We observe first that this case does not involve an attempt by Congress to increase its own powers at the expense of the Executive Branch. . . .

Similarly, we do not think the Act works any *judicial* usurpation of properly executive functions. . . . [The Special Division] may only [appoint an independent counsel] upon the specific request of the Attorney General. . . .

Finally, we do not think that the Act "impermissibly undermines" the powers of the Executive Branch, . . . or "disrupts the proper balance between the coordinate branches." . . . It is undeniable that the Act reduces the amount of control or supervision that the Attorney General and, through him, the President exercise over investigation and prosecution of a certain class of alleged criminal activity. The Attorney General is not allowed to appoint the individual of his choice; he does not determine the counsel's jurisdiction; and his power to remove a counsel is limited. . . . Notwithstanding the fact that the counsel is to some degree "independent" and free from Executive supervision to a greater extent than other federal prosecutors, in our view, these features of the Act [permitting removal by the Attorney General "for cause" and making the Attorney General initiate the original appointment] give the Executive Branch sufficient control over the independent counsel to ensure that the President is able to perform his constitutionally assigned duties. . . .

Justice SCALIA, dissenting:

. . . .

That is what this suit is about. Power. The allocation of power among Congress, the President and the courts in such fashion as to preserve the

equilibrium the Constitution sought to establish—so that "a gradual concentration of the several powers in the same department" . . . can effectively be resisted. Frequently an issue of this sort will come before the Court clad, so to speak, in sheep's clothing: the potential of the asserted principle to effect important change in the equilibrium of power is not immediately evident, and must be discerned by a careful and perceptive analysis. But this wolf comes as a wolf. . . .

II

. . . .

To repeat, Article II, [section 1] of the Constitution provides:

> "The executive Power shall be vested in a President of the United States."

As I described at the outset of this opinion, this does not mean *some of* the executive power, but *all of* the executive power. It seems to me, therefore, that the decision of the Court of Appeals invalidating the present statute must be upheld on fundamental separation-of-powers principles if the following two questions are answered affirmatively: (1) Is the conduct of a criminal prosecution (and of an investigation to decide whether to prosecute) the exercise of purely executive power? (2) Does the statute deprive the President of the United States of exclusive control over the exercise of that power? Surprising to say, the Court appears to concede an affirmative answer to both questions, but seeks to avoid the inevitable conclusion that since the statute vests some purely executive power in a person who is not President of the United States it is void. . . .

The utter incompatibility of the Court's approach with our constitutional traditions can be made more clear, perhaps, by applying it to the powers of the other two Branches. Is it conceivable that if Congress passed a statute depriving itself of less than full and entire control over some insignificant area of legislation, we would inquire whether the matter was "*so central* to the functioning of the Legislative Branch" as really to require complete control, or whether the statute gives Congress "*sufficient* control over the surrogate legislator to ensure that Congress is able to perform its constitutionally assigned duties"? Of course we would have none of that. Once we determined that a purely legislative power was at issue, we would require it to be exercised, wholly and entirely, by Congress. . . .

Is it unthinkable that the President should have such exclusive power, even when alleged crimes by him or his close associates are at issue? No more so than that Congress should have the exclusive power of legislation, even when what is at issue is its own exemption from the burdens of certain laws. . . .

The Court has, nonetheless, replaced the clear constitutional prescription that the executive power belongs to the President with a "balancing test." . . . Once we depart from the text of the Constitution, just where short of [an entirely weakened executive] do we stop? The most amazing feature of the Court's opinion is that it does not even purport to give an answer. It simply *announces,* with no analysis, that the ability to control the decision whether to investigate and prosecute the President's closest advisors, and indeed the President himself, is not "so central to the functioning of the Executive Branch" as to be constitutionally required to be within the President's control. . . .

Besides weakening the Presidency by reducing the zeal of his staff, it must also be obvious that the institution of independent counsel enfeebles him more directly in his constant confrontations with Congress by eroding his public support. Nothing is so politically effective as the ability to charge that one's opponent and his associates are not merely wrongheaded, naive, ineffective, but, in all probability, "crooks." . . . The present statute provides ample means for that sort of attack, assuring that massive and lengthy investigations will occur. . . .

V

The purpose of the separation and equilibrium of powers in general, and of the unitary Executive in particular, was not merely to assure effective government but to preserve individual freedom. . . .

Under our system of government, the primary check against prosecutorial abuse is a political one. The prosecutors who exercise this awesome discretion are selected and can be removed by a president, whom the people have trusted enough to elect. Moreover, when crimes are not investigated and prosecuted fairly, nonselectively, with a reasonable sense of proportion, the President pays the cost in political damage to his administration. . . .

I cannot imagine that there are not many thoughtful men and women in Congress who realize that the benefits of this legislation are far outweighed by its harmful effect upon our system of government, and even upon the nature of justice received by those men and women who agree to serve in the executive branch. But it is difficult to vote to repeal a statute called, appropriately enough, the Ethics in Government Act. If Congress is controlled by one party other than the one to which the President belongs, it has little incentive to repeal it; if it is controlled by the same party, it dare not. By its shortsighted action today, I fear the Court has permanently encumbered the Republic with an institution that will do it great harm.

MISTRETTA v. UNITED STATES

109 S. Ct. 647 (1989)

Justice BLACKMUN delivered the opinion of court [joined by Justices BRENNAN, KENNEDY, MARSHALL, O'CONNOR, STEVENS, and WHITE, and Chief Justice REHNQUIST]:

In this litigation, we . . . consider the constitutionality of the Sentencing Guidelines promulgated by the United States Sentencing Commission. The Commission is a body created under the Sentencing Reform Act of 1984. . . .

I

A

Background

For almost a century, the Federal Government employed in criminal cases a system of indeterminate sentencing. Statutes specified the penalties for crimes but nearly always gave the sentencing judge wide discretion to decide whether the offender should be incarcerated and for how long, whether he should be fined and how much, and whether some lesser restraint, such as probation, should be imposed instead of imprisonment and fine. . . .

Historically, federal sentencing—the function of determining the scope and extent of punishment—never has been thought to be assigned by the Constitution to the exclusive jurisdiction of any one of the three Branches of government. . . . Congress delegated almost unfettered discretion to the sentencing judge to determine what the sentence should be within the customarily wide range so selected. The broad discretion was further enhanced by the power later granted the judge to suspend the sentence and by the resulting growth of an elaborate probation system. Also, with the advent of parole, Congress moved toward a "three-way sharing" of sentencing responsibility by granting correction personnel in the Executive Branch the discretion to release a prisoner before the expiration of the sentence imposed by the judge. Thus, under the indeterminate-sentence system, Congress defined the maximum, the judge imposed a sentence within a statutory range (which it usually could replace with probation), and the Executive Branch's parole official eventually determined the actual duration of imprisonment. . . .

Serious disparities in sentences, however, were common. Rehabilitation as a sound penological theory came to be questioned and, in any event, was regarded by some as an unattainable goal for most cases. . . .

[After several reform efforts from the 1950s through the 1970s,] [f]undamental and widespread dissatisfaction with the uncertainties and the disparities continued to be expressed. Congress had wrestled with the problem for more than a decade when, in 1984, it enacted the sweeping reforms that are at issue here. . . .

Before settling on a mandatory-guideline system, Congress considered other competing proposals for sentencing reform. It rejected strict determinate sentencing because it concluded that a guideline system would be successful in reducing sentence disparities while retaining the flexibility needed to adjust for unanticipated factors arising in a particular case. . . . The Judiciary Committee rejected a proposal that would have made the sentencing guidelines only advisory. . . .

B

The Act

The Act, as adopted, revises the old sentencing process in several ways:

. . .

2. It consolidates the power that had been exercised by the sentencing judge and the Parole Commission to decide what punishment an offender should suffer. This is done by creating the United States Sentencing Commission, directing that Commission to devise guidelines to be used for sentencing, and prospectively abolishing the Parole Commission. . . .

4. It makes the Sentencing Commission's guidelines binding on the courts, although it preserves for the judge the discretion to depart from the guidelines applicable to a particular case if the judge finds an aggravating or mitigating factor present the Commission did not adequately consider when formulating the guidelines. . . . The Act also requires the court to state its reasons for the sentence imposed and to give the "specific reason" for imposing a sentence different from that described in the guideline . . . .

C

The Sentencing Commission

The Commission is established "as an independent commission in the judicial branch of the United States." . . . It has seven voting members (one of whom is the Chairman) appointed by the President "by and with the advice and consent of the Senate." "At least three of the members shall be Federal judges selected after considering a list of six judges recommended to the President by the Judicial Conference of the United States." No more than four members of the Commission shall be members of the same political party. The Attorney General, or his designee, is an ex officio non-voting member. The Chairman and other members of the Commission are subject to removal by the President "only for neglect of duty or malfeasance in office or for other good cause shown." . . . Except for initial staggering of terms, a voting member serves for six years and may not serve more than two full terms. . . .

D

The Responsibilities of the Commission

In addition to the duty the Commission has to promulgate determinative-sentence guidelines, it is under an obligation periodically to "review and revise" the guidelines. . . .

We note, in passing, that the monitoring function [of the Commission] is not without its burden. Every year, with respect to each of more than 40,000 sentences, the federal courts must forward and the Commission must review, the presentence report, the guideline worksheets, and the tribunal's sentencing statement, and any written plea agreement.

II

This Litigation

On Dec. 10, 1987, John M. Mistretta (petitioner) and another were indicted in the United States District Court for the Western District of Missouri on three counts centering in a cocaine sale. . . . Mistretta moved to have the promulgated Guidelines ruled unconstitutional on the grounds that the Sentencing Commission was constituted in violation of the established doctrine of separation of powers, and that Congress delegated excessive authority to the Commission to structure the Guidelines. As has been noted, the District Court was not persuaded by these contentions. . . .

III

Delegation of Power

Petitioner argues that in delegating the power to promulgate sentencing guidelines for every federal criminal offense to an independent Sentencing Commission, Congress has granted the Commission excessive legislative discretion in violation of the constitutionally based nondelegation doctrine. We do not agree.

The nondelegation doctrine is rooted in the principle of separation of powers that underlies our tripartite system of government. The Constitution provides that "[a]ll legislative Powers herein granted shall be vested in a Congress of the United States." . . . We also have recognized, however, that the separation-of-powers principle, and the nondelegation doctrine in particular, do not prevent Congress from obtaining the assistance of its coordinate Branches. . . . So long as Congress "shall lay down by legislative act an intelligible principle to which the person or body authorized to [exercise the delegated authority] is directed to conform, such legislative action is not a forbidden delegation of legislative power." . . .

Applying this "intelligible principle" test to congressional delegations, our jurisprudence has been driven by a practical understanding that in our increasingly complex society, replete with ever changing and more technical problems, Congress simply cannot do its job absent an ability to delegate power under broad general directives. . . .

In light of our approval of [other] broad delegations, we harbor no doubt that Congress' delegation of authority to the Sentencing Commission is sufficiently specific and detailed to meet constitutional requirements. . . .

We cannot dispute petitioner's contention that the Commission enjoys significant discretion in formulating guidelines. The Commission does have discretionary authority to determine the relative severity of federal crimes and to assess the relative weight of the offender characteristics that Congress listed for the Commission to consider. . . .

But our cases do not at all suggest that delegations of this type may not carry with them the need to exercise judgment on matters of policy. . . .

IV

Separation of Powers

. . . .

This Court consistently has given voice to, and has reaffirmed, the central judgment of the Framers of the Constitution that, within our political scheme, the separation of governmental powers into three coordinate Branches is essential to the preservation of liberty. . . .

In applying the principle of separated powers in our jurisprudence, we have sought to give life to Madison's view of the appropriate relationship among the three coequal Branches. . . . [T]he Framers did not require—and indeed rejected—the notion that the three Branches must be entirely separate and distinct. . . . Separation of powers, [Madison] wrote, "d[oes] not mean that these [three] departments ought to have no *partial agency* in, or no *control* over the acts of each other," but rather "that where the *whole* power of one department is exercised by the same hands which possess the *whole* power of another department, the fundamental principles of a free constitution, are subverted" (emphasis in original). . . . In a passage now commonplace in our cases, Justice Jackson summarized the pragmatic, flexible view of the differentiated governmental power to which we are heir:

> "While the Constitution diffuses power the better to secure liberty, it also contemplates that practice will integrate the dispersed powers into a workable government. It enjoins upon its branches separateness but interdependence, autonomy but reciprocity." *Youngstown Sheet & Tube Co., v. Sawyer,* . . . (1952) (concurring opinion).

In adopting this flexible understanding of separation of powers, we simply have recognized Madison's teaching that the greatest security against tyranny—the accumulation of excessive authority in a single branch—lies not in a hermetic division between the Branches, but in a carefully crafted system of checked and balanced power within each Branch. . . .

. . . In cases specifically involving the Judicial Branch, we have expressed our vigilance against two dangers: first, that the Judicial Branch neither be assigned nor allowed "tasks that are more appropriately accomplished by [other] branches," . . . and, second, that no provision of law "impermissibly threatens the institutional integrity of the Judicial Branch." . . .

. . . Although the unique composition and responsibilities of the Sentencing Commission give rise to serious concerns about a disruption of the appropriate balance of governmental power among the coordinate Branches, we conclude, upon close inspection, that petitioner's fears for the fundamental structural protections of the Constitution prove, at least in this case, to be "more smoke than fire," and do not compel us to invalidate Congress' considered scheme for resolving the seemingly intractable dilemma of excessive disparity in criminal sentencing.

A

Location of the Commission

The Sentencing Commission unquestionably is a peculiar institution within the framework of our Government. Although placed by the Act in the Judicial Branch, it is not a court and does not exercise judicial power. Rather, the Commission is an "independent" body comprised of seven voting members including at least three federal judges, entrusted by Congress with the primary task of promulgating sentencing guidelines. . . . Our constitutional principles of separated powers are not violated, however, by mere anomaly or innovation. . . . As a general principle, we stated as recently as last Term that " 'executive or administrative duties of a nonjudicial nature may not be imposed on judges holding office under Article III of the Constitution.' " . . .

Nonetheless, we have recognized significant exceptions to this general rule and have approved the assumption of some nonadjudicatory activities by the Judicial Branch. In keeping with Justice Jackson's *Youngstown* admonition that the separation of powers contemplates the integration of dispersed powers into a workable government, we have recognized the constitutionality of a "twilight area" in which the activities of the separate Branches merge. . . .

In light of this precedent and practice, we can discern no separation-of-powers impediment to the placement of the Sentencing Commission within the Judicial Branch. . . .

Given the consistent responsibility of federal judges to pronounce sentence within the statutory range established by Congress, we find that the role of the Commission in promulgating guidelines for the exercise of that judicial function bears considerable similarity to the role of this Court in establishing rules of procedure under the various enabling acts. . . .

We do not believe, however, that the significantly political nature of the Commission's work renders unconstitutional its placement within the Judicial Branch. Our separation-of-powers analysis does not turn on the labelling of an activity as "substantive" as opposed to "procedural," or "political" as opposed to "judicial." . . . Rather, our inquiry is focused on the "unique aspects of the congressional plan at issue and its practical consequences in light of the larger concerns that underlie Article III." . . . In this case, the "practical consequences" of locating the Commission within the Judicial Branch pose no threat of undermining the integrity of the Judicial Branch or of expanding the powers of the Judiciary beyond constitutional bounds by uniting within the Branch the political or quasi-legislative power of the Commission with the judicial power of the courts. . . .

B

Composition of the Commission

. . . .

. . . We find Congress' requirement of judicial service somewhat troublesome, but we do not believe that the Act impermissibly interferes with the functioning of the Judiciary. . . .

... The Act does not conscript judges for the Commission. No Commission member to date has been appointed without [the member's] consent and we have no reason to believe that the Act confers upon the President any authority to force a judge to serve on the Commission against his will. ...

Moreover, we cannot see how the service of federal judges on the Commission will have a constitutionally significant practical effect on the operation of the Judicial Branch. We see no reason why service on the Commission should result in widespread judicial recusals. ...

We are somewhat more troubled by petitioner's argument that the Judiciary's entanglement in the political work of the Commission undermines public confidence in the disinterestedness of the Judicial Branch. While the problem of individual bias is usually cured through recusal, no such mechanism can overcome the appearance of institutional partiality that may arise from judiciary involvement in the making of policy. The legitimacy of the Judicial Branch ultimately depends on its reputation for impartiality and nonpartisanship. That reputation may not be borrowed by the political Branches to cloak their own work in the neutral colors of judicial action.

Although it is a judgment that is not without difficulty, we conclude that the participation of federal judges on the Sentencing Commission does not threaten, either in fact or in appearance, the impartiality of the Judicial Branch. We are drawn to this conclusion by one paramount consideration: that the Sentencing Commission is devoted exclusively to the development of rules to rationalize a process that has been and will continue to be performed exclusively by the Judicial Branch. In our view, this is an essentially neutral endeavor and one in which judicial participation is peculiarly appropriate. ...

Justice SCALIA dissenting:

... I dissent from today's decision because I can find no place within our constitutional system for an agency created by Congress to exercise no governmental power other than the making of laws.

I

. . . .

It should be apparent from the above that the decisions made by the Commission are far from technical, but are heavily laden (or ought to be) with value judgments and policy assessments. ...

II

Precisely because the scope of delegation is largely uncontrollable by the courts, we must be particularly rigorous in preserving the Constitution's structural restrictions that deter excessive delegation. The major one, it seems to me, is that the power to make law cannot be exercised by anyone other than Congress, except in conjunction with the lawful exercise of executive or judicial power. . . .

. . . In the present case, however, a pure delegation of legislative power is precisely what we have before us. It is irrelevant whether the standards are adequate, because they are not standards related to the exercise of executive or judicial powers; they are, plainly and simply, standards for further legislation. . . .

. . . The power to make law at issue here, in other words, is not ancillary but quite naked. The situation is no different in principle from what would exist if Congress gave the same power of writing sentencing laws to a congressional agency such as the General Accounting Office, or to members of its staff. . . .

By reason of today's decision, I anticipate that Congress will find delegation of its lawmaking powers much more attractive in the future. If rulemaking can be entirely unrelated to the exercise of judicial or executive powers, I foresee all manner of "expert" bodies, insulated from the political process, to which Congress will delegate various portions of its lawmaking responsibility. . . .

III

. . . .

Today's decision may aptly be described as the *Humphrey's Executor* of the Judicial Branch, and I think we will live to regret it. Henceforth there may be agencies "within the Judicial Branch" (whatever that means), exercising governmental powers, that are neither courts nor controlled by courts, nor even controlled by judges. If an "independent agency" such as this can be given the power to fix sentences previously exercised by district courts, I must assume that a similar agency can be given the powers to adopt Rules of Procedure and Rules of Evidence previously exercised by this Court. The bases for distinction would be thin indeed.

Today's decision follows a regrettable tendency of our recent separation-of-powers jurisprudence . . . to treat the Constitution as though it were no more than a generalized prescription that the functions of the Branches should not be commingled too much—how much is too much to be determined, case-by-case, by this Court. The Constitution is not that. Rather, as its name suggests, it is a prescribed structure, a framework, for the conduct of government. In designing the structure, the framers *themselves* considered how much commingling was, in the generality of things, acceptable, and set forth their conclusions in the document. . . .

I think the Court errs, in other words, not so much because it mistakes the degree of commingling, but because it fails to recognize that this case is not about commingling, but about the creation of a new branch altogether, a sort of junior-varsity Congress. It may well be that in some circumstances such a branch would be desirable; perhaps the agency before us here will prove to be so. But there are many desirable dispositions that do not accord with the constitutional structure we live under. And in the long run the improvisation of a constitutional structure on the basis of currently perceived utility will be disastrous. . . .

Questions

1. Does congressional removal power over the Comptroller General by joint resolution (i.e., resolution passed by both houses of Congress and presented to the President for signature or veto) give Congress "control" over the actions of the Comptroller General?
2. In *Bowsher*, is Justice White correct in claiming that, in reality, it is more difficult to remove the Comptroller General by joint resolution than to impeach him? Should the Court consider this practical argument in deciding the case?
3. In his conclusion, what did Justice White mean by saying that the Court was "insensitive" to its proper constitutional role?
4. What is Justice Blackmun's argument in *Bowsher*? What is the proper role of a court when confronted with the choice posed by Blackmun? Could the Court have followed Blackmun's recommendations?
5. Are the decisions in *Morrison* and *Mistretta* consistent with the theory and tone of the opinion in *Bowsher*? If the decisions are not consistent, why did the Court's position change?
6. Did any changes in the composition of the Supreme Court affect the decisions in *Morrison* and *Mistretta* when compared to the opinion in *Bowsher*?
7. In *Morrison*, the majority says that the "real question" is whether the independent counsel law "impede[s]" the President's ability to perform his constitutional duty. Did the Budget Deficit Control Act "impede" Congress or the President from performing their duties? Is your response affected by the fact that both Congress and the President approved the Act?
8. Should judicial officers be involved in the process of appointing officials who perform executive branch functions?
9. The shadow of Watergate hangs over the independent counsel statute. The statute's design was influenced by the fact that special prosecutor Archibald Cox was fired in the middle of his investigation when he pursued materials that President Nixon sought to hide. Do you detect an awareness of Wa-

tergate either explicitly or implicitly in the majority opinion in *Morrison?* Could an underlying awareness of the specific problems from Watergate explain any differences in the decisions in *Bowsher* and *Morrison?*

10. If Congress had passed the Deficit Control Act in response to a severe national recession caused by the federal budget deficit, do you think that the Court's decision in *Bowsher* would have been different?

11. Do you detect any sensitivity to Watergate in Justice Scalia's dissenting opinion in *Morrison?*

12. Justice Scalia asserts in *Morrison* that permitting the President to investigate himself is no different than permitting Congress to exempt itself from certain laws (e.g., Congress does not apply federal labor laws to its own employees). Are there any differences in the structure and composition of these branches of government that undercut Scalia's argument? Is a criminal investigation of White House activities analogous to a statutory exemption for Congress?

13. In *Morrison,* is Justice Scalia correct in asserting that the people will keep the President accountable if he does not pursue criminal investigations and prosecutions within the executive branch?

14. How can the Court quote James Madison in the Federalist Papers and Justice Jackson's *Youngstown* opinion to emphasize the supreme importance of separation of powers in *Bowsher* and then quote the same two sources to justify a "pragmatic, flexible view" of separation of powers in *Mistretta?* How malleable are the sources of authority utilized by the Supreme Court?

15. Do Court opinions follow from the application of legal theories? Alternatively, are Court opinions merely rationalizations for whatever results the justices desire to reach in each case?

THREE

The Justices and the Power
of the Judiciary

The Constitution defines the structure of the federal government. If there is a dispute about the definition and allocation of power among the branches of government, federal judges, as the ultimate interpreters of the Constitution, determine the extent of each branch's authority. If there is a dispute about the extent of judicial power, the Supreme Court is placed in the difficult position of defining its own power and that of other courts. In order to preserve the judiciary's image and legitimacy, the justices must maintain the power of the courts and, if possible, simultaneously avoid political battles with the other government branches. Obedience to judicial decisions depends substantially upon voluntary acquiescence and cooperative enforcements efforts from the executive branch, both of which stem from acceptance of the judiciary's actions as legitimate, legal decisions. Excessive conflicts and confrontations with other political actors create risks that the relative weakness of the courts' practical enforcement powers will be revealed. Thus, the judiciary's unique ability to define its own power is shaped, in part, by the justices' consideration of the political consequences of their decisions.

Americans think of themselves as living in a "democracy." Consistent with democratic ideals, the Constitution establishes a system of government emphasizing citizen participation in the governing process through free elections. Thus, the electoral process permits citizens to maintain accountability and control over their government leaders. If the citizens disagree with decisions by legislators or the president, they can elect new leaders at the next election.

The federal judiciary, however, is removed from direct accountability. Because federal judges serve "during good behavior," or essentially for life, the citizens cannot use their votes to remove judges from office, even when the judges' decisions are highly unpopular. Some commentators argue that the broad authority to influence public policy possessed by the unaccountable judges constitutes an "undemocratic" aspect of the American governing system. By narrowly defining "democracy" as citizen control over government, this argument presumes that only elected officials are legitimate policy makers. The Constitution, by contrast, employs a broader conception of democracy.

The Constitution recognizes that if all elements of government were directly accountable to the electorate, there would be a great risk of tyranny by the majority. Any majority of voters could always work its will to the detriment of political minorities. To counter these risks, the Bill of Rights provides protections for individuals' rights, and these protections create limitations upon the power of electoral majorities to dictate public policy. For example, a majority of citizens may seek to suppress unpopular opinions, but the First Amendment protects those who wish to express minority viewpoints.

Federal judges are insulated from direct accountability in order to give them the security to make courageous, anti-majoritarian decisions. The federal judges are responsible for upholding the Bill of Rights' protections for individuals and political minorities. Thus, the Constitution, by creating an independent judiciary and a Bill of Rights, defines democracy as citizen participation in government *plus* the protection of individuals' rights. In the most famous historical example, although a majority of voters in many southern states favored racial discrimination and segregation in the 1950s, federal judges issued decisions that changed public policy against the wishes of the electoral majorities in order to protect the rights of African-Americans. The constitutional conception of democracy embodied in the Fourteenth Amendment's Equal Protection Clause overrode definitions of democracy that emphasized simple majority rule.

Because federal judges are not directly accountable to the voters, there are risks that they may act dictatorially in making decisions according to their own preferences and values. According to Gary McDowell, many judicial decisions "have more to do with the individual notions of justice embraced by the justices and judges than with the Constitution."[1] The threat of inappropriate and excessive judicial actions is an inherent risk in a system which grants judges independence and broad authority.

1. Gary L. McDowell, *Curbing the Courts: The Constitution and the Limits of Judicial Power* (Baton Rouge, LA: Louisiana State University Press, 1988), p. 3.

This risk is exacerbated by the fact that the judiciary has the authority to define its own power in the course of interpreting the Constitution. What prevents federal judges from becoming dictators who control public policy?

Several practical factors limit the risks of judicial tyranny. First, although judges are not directly accountable to the voters, the electorate indirectly affects the composition of the judiciary. By electing a new president, the voters can change the judiciary because the president will gradually replace departing judges with new appointees who share the president's values. Although political conservatives criticize the judiciary for going "too far" in decisions affecting public policies, in fact, during the 1980s President Reagan managed to replace nearly half of the federal judiciary with conservative appointees. The interaction of political forces within the American governing system tends to prevent any institutions, including the courts, from straying too far or too long from the evolving mainstream values.

This limitation on judicial power is not quick or direct, but over time the composition of the judiciary will reflect trends in national electoral politics. The composition of the courts, however, will never precisely mirror the trends in electoral politics. On the Supreme Court in 1990, for example, two-thirds of the justices came from the Republican party. By 1991, after the retirements of Justices William Brennan and Thurgood Marshall, only one justice remained from the Democratic party. Republican domination of the presidency during the 1970s, 1980s, and early 1990s gradually created an almost entirely Republican Supreme Court, although only a minority of American voters declare themselves affiliated with that party and American voters consistently elect Democrats to Congress and other political offices. Despite the imprecise and indirect effects of elections upon the composition of the judiciary, the appointment process and its relationship to the electoral process make it unlikely that many judges will be outside the mainstream of American political values. Being in the mainstream, however, leaves plenty of room for disagreement among the judges because American society lacks a clear consensus on many controversial issues (e.g., abortion). The moderating effects of the political process prevent extremism but do not guarantee agreement on all issues facing society.

Second, as chapter 7 will discuss, unpopular judicial decisions lead to reactions from other political actors. The effects of unpopular judicial decisions are frequently slowed or changed through resistance by government officials or the public. As Charles Johnson and Bradley Canon explain, "Like the Congress, the Supreme Court and lower courts must rely on others to translate policy into action. . . . [T]he process of translating [judicial] decisions into action is often a political one subject to a variety of pressures from . . . political actors in the system."[2] Moreover, Congress and the President can react to judicial decisions by proposing constitutional amendments and legislation that will limit judicial authority. Although this is not an instantaneous check upon the judiciary, the threat of altering the courts' jurisdiction and other aspects of judicial power is constantly present. As illustrated by the quick congressional reaction to *Texas v. Johnson* in 1989, namely writing a new statute to prosecute people who burn the American flag (see chapter 7), if judicial decisions are sufficiently unpopular, the legislature may be able to react relatively quickly.

Third, because of the relative weakness of the judiciary, judges will frequently restrain themselves in order to avoid confrontations with the other governmental branches. Courts can avoid controversies by manipulating jurisdictional rules. For example, the court may declare that a litigant lacks "standing," and thereby decline to recognize the litigant as a proper party to pursue a case. Although the reasons for such decisions will always be expressed in principled terms which usually emphasize the need for a limited judicial role in public policy matters, judges' underlying motivations deserve critical scrutiny and analysis. Judges may actually avoid controversial issues in order to prevent confrontations with other political actors. In the cases concerning the Vietnam War reprinted in this chapter, the Supreme Court asserts the "political question" doctrine in order to avoid becoming entangled in a difficult foreign policy matter. The justices claim that policy decisions on such issues must be reserved for elected officials, but their actions in avoiding the cases must also be analyzed in light of the Constitution's words and the practical political consequences of a potential Supreme Court decision.

Although the Supreme Court may avoid some controversies that might threaten its image, legitimacy, and power, the justices must simultaneously ensure that they protect judicial authority in the face of challenges. The Supreme Court must maintain the judiciary's ability to interpret the Constitution authoritatively and to protect the rights of individuals. In the Supreme Court cases that follow (*Stump v. Sparkman, Spallone v. United States,* and *Missouri v. Jenkins*), the justices make strong statements in support of judicial authority. At the same time, there are signs that the justices carefully seek to establish an appropriate balance between maintaining needed court authority and avoiding excessive judicial power. This is a difficult balance to achieve. The Court's decisions on these difficult issues frequently elicit significant disagreement among the justices themselves.

2. Charles A. Johnson and Bradley C. Canon, *Judicial Policies: Implementation and Impact,* (Washington, D.C.: Congressional Quarterly Press, 1984), p. 4.

MORA v. McNAMARA

389 U.S. 934 (1967)

Petition for writ of certiorari to the United States Court of Appeals for the District of Columbia Circuit.

Nov. 6, 1967. Denied.

Justice MARSHALL took no part in the consideration or decision of this petition.

Justice STEWART, with whom Justice DOUGLAS joins, dissenting:

The petitioners were drafted into the United States Army in late 1965, and six months later were ordered to a West Coast replacement station for shipment to Vietnam. They brought this suit to prevent the Secretary of Defense and the Secretary of the Army from carrying out those orders, and requested a declaratory judgment that the present United States military activity in Vietnam is "illegal." The District Court dismissed the suit, and the Court of Appeals affirmed.

There exist in this case questions of great magnitude. Some are akin to those referred to by Justice Douglas in Mitchell v. United States, 386 U.S. 972. . . . But there are others:

I. Is the present United States military activity in Vietnam a "war" within the meaning of Article I, Section 8, Clause 11 of the Constitution?

II. If so, may the Executive constitutionally order the petitioners to participate in that military activity, when no war has been declared by the Congress?

III. Of what relevance to Question II is the Joint Congressional ("Tonkin Bay") Resolution of August 10, 1964?

(a) Do present United States military operations fall within the terms of the Joint Resolution?

(b) If the Joint Resolution purports to give the Chief Executive authority to commit United States forces to armed conflict limited in scope only by his own absolute discretion, is the Resolution a constitutionally impermissible delegation of all or part of Congress' power to declare war?

These are large and deeply troubling questions. Whether the Court would ultimately reach them depends, of course, upon the resolution of serious preliminary issues of justiciability. We cannot make these problems go away simply by refusing to hear the case of three obscure Army privates. I intimate not even tentative views upon any of these matters, but I think the Court should squarely face them by granting certiorari and setting this case for oral argument.

Justice DOUGLAS, with whom Justice STEWART concurs, dissenting:

. . . .

A host of problems is raised. Does the President's authority to repel invasions and quiet insurrections, his powers in foreign relations and his duty to execute faithfully the laws of the United States, including its treaties, justify what has been threatened of petitioners? What is the relevancy of the Gulf of Tonkin Resolution and the yearly appropriations in support of the Vietnam effort? . . .

We do not, of course, sit as a committee of oversight or supervision. What resolutions the President asks and what the Congress provides are not our concern. With respect to the Federal Government, we sit only to decide actual cases or controversies within judicial cognizance that arise as a result of what the Congress or the President or a judge does or attempts to do to a person or his property. . . .

These petitioners should be told whether their case is beyond judicial cognizance. If it is not, we should then reach the merits of their claims, on which I intimate no views whatsoever.

HOLTZMAN v. SCHLESINGER

414 U.S. 1304 (1973)
(August 1, 1973)

Justice MARSHALL, [sitting alone as] Circuit Justice:

This case is before me on an application to vacate a stay entered by a three-judge panel of the United States Court of Appeals for the Second Circuit. Applicants, a Congresswoman from New York and several Air Force officers serving in Asia, brought this action to enjoin continued United States air operations over Cambodia. They argue that such military activity has not been authorized by Congress and that, absent such authorization, it violates Art. I, [section] 8, [clause] 11 of the Constitution. The United States District Court agreed and . . . permanently enjoined respondents, the Secretary of Defense, the Acting Secretary of the Air Force, and the Deputy Secretary of Defense, from "participating in any way in military activities in or over Cambodia or releasing any bombs which may fall in Cambodia." However, the effective date of the injunction was delayed until July 27, 1973, in order to give respondents an opportunity to apply to the Court of Appeals for a stay pending appeal. Respondents promptly applied for such a stay, and the application was granted, without opinion, on July 27. Applicants then filed this motion to vacate the stay. For the reasons stated below, I am unable to say that the Court of Appeals abused its discretion in staying the District Court's order. In view of the complexity and importance of the issues involved and the absence of authoritative precedent, it would be inappropriate for me, acting as a single Circuit Justice to vacate the order of the Court of Appeals.

I

Since the facts of this dispute are on the public record . . . [i]t suffices to note that publicly acknowledged United States involvement in the Cambodian hostilities began with the President's announcement on April 30, 1970, that this country was launching attacks "to clean out major enemy sanctuaries on the Cambodian-Vietnam border," and that American military action in that country has since met with gradually increasing congressional resistance.

Although United States ground troops had been withdrawn from the Cambodian theater by June 30, 1970, in the summer of that year Congress enacted the so called Fulbright Proviso prohibiting the use of funds for military support of Cambodia. . . .

II

. . . [A]pplicants forcefully contend that continued United States military activity in Cambodia is illegal. Specifically, they argue that the President is constitutionally disabled in nonemergency situations from exercising the warmaking power in the absence of some affirmative action by Congress. . . .

. . . Some may greet with considerable skepticism the claim that vital security interests of our country rest on whether the Air Force is permitted to continue bombing for a few more days, particularly in light of respondents' failure to produce affidavits from any responsible Government official asserting that such irreparable injury will occur. But it cannot be denied that the assessment of such injury poses the most sensitive of problems, about which Justices of this Court have little or no information or expertise. While we have undoubted authority to judge the legality of executive action, we are on treacherous ground indeed when we attempt judgments as to its wisdom or necessity. . . .

. . . [I]f the decision were mine alone, I might well conclude on the merits that continued American military operations in Cambodia are un-constitutional. But the Supreme Court is a collegial institution, and its decisions reflect the views of a majority of the sitting Justices. It follows that when I sit in my capacity as a Circuit Justice, I act not for myself alone but as a surrogate for the entire Court, from whence my ultimate authority in these matters derives. A Circuit Justice therefore bears a heavy responsibility to conscientiously reflect the views of his Brethren as best he perceives them, . . . and this responsibility is particularly press-ing when, as now, the Court is not in session.

When the problem is viewed from this perspective, it is immeasur-ably complicated. It must be recognized that we are writing on an almost entirely clean slate in this area. . . .

Lurking in this suit are questions of standing, judicial competence, and substantive constitutional law which go to the roots of the division of power in a constitutional democracy. These are the sort of issues which should not be decided precipitately or without the benefit of proper con-sultation. . . .

. . . In light of the complexity and importance of the issues posed, I cannot say that the Court of Appeals abused its discretion.

When the final history of the Cambodian War is written, it is unlikely to make pleasant reading. The decision to send American troops "to dis-tant lands to die of foreign fevers and foreign shot and shell," . . . may ultimately be adjudged to have been not only unwise but also unlawful.

But the proper response to an arguably illegal action is not lawless-ness by judges charged with interpreting and enforcing the laws. Down that road lies tyranny and repression. We have a government of limited powers, and those limits pertain to the Justices of this Court as well as to Congress and the Executive. Our Constitution assures that the law will ultimately prevail, but it also requires that the law be applied in accor-dance with lawful procedures. . . .

HOLTZMAN v. SCHLESINGER

414 U.S. 1316 (1973)
(August 3, 1973)

Justice DOUGLAS, [sitting alone as] Circuit Justice:

. . . .

An application for stay denied by one Justice may be made to another. We do not, however, encourage the practice; and when the Term starts, the Justices all being in Washington, D.C., the practice is to refer the sec-ond application to the entire Court. That is the desirable practice to dis-courage "shopping around."

When the Court is in recess that practice cannot be followed, for the Justices are scattered. . . .

My brother MARSHALL accurately points out that if the foreign policy goals of this Government are to be weighed the Judiciary is probably the least qualified branch of the government to weigh them. He also states that if stays by judicial officers in cases of this kind are to be vacated the circumstances must be "exceptional." I agree with those premises, and I respect [Justice MARSHALL's] views. . . .

But this case in its stark realities involves the grim consequences of a capital case. The classic capital case is whether Mr. Lew, Mr. Low, or Mr. Lucas should die. The present case involves whether Mr. X (an unknown person or persons) should die. No one knows who they are. They may be Cambodian farmers whose only "sin" is to desire socialized medicine to alleviate the suffering of their families and neighbors. Or Mr. X may be the American pilot or navigator who drops a ton of bombs on a Cambodian village. The upshot is that we know that someone is about to die. . . .

. . . The basic question on the merits is whether Congress, within the meaning of Article I, [section] 8, [clause] 11, has "declared war" in Cambodia.

It has become popular to think the President has that power to declare war. But there is not a word in the Constitution that grants that power to him. It runs only to Congress. . . .

The question of justiciability does not seem substantial. . . . In my time we held that President Truman in the undeclared Korean war had no power to seize the steel mills in order to increase war production. *Youngstown Sheet & Tube Co. v. Sawyer.* . . . The *Prize Cases* and the *Youngstown* case involved the seizure of property. But the Government conceded on oral argument that property is no more important than life under our Constitution. Our Fifth Amendment which curtails federal power under the Due Process Clause protects "life, liberty, or property" in that order. Property is important, but if Truman could not seize it in violation of the Constitution I do not see how any President can take "life" in violation of the Constitution. . . .

. . . Some say [the Cambodian conflict] is merely an extension of the "war" in Vietnam, a "war" which the Second Circuit has held in *Berk v. Laird* . . . to raise a "political" question, not a justiciable one. I have had serious doubts about the correctness of that decision, but our Court has never passed on the question authoritatively. . . . The merits of the present controversy are therefore, to say the least, substantial, since denial of the application before me would catapult our airmen as well as Cambodian peasants into the death zone. I do what I think any judge would do in a capital case—vacate the stay entered by the Court of Appeals. . . .

SCHLESINGER v. HOLTZMAN

414 U.S. 1321 (1973)
(August 4, 1973)

Justice MARSHALL [sitting alone as] Circuit Justice:

. . . .

In the ordinary course, a Justice acting as Circuit Justice would defer with respect to a District Court order until the Court of Appeals had acted, but in the present circumstances the Court of Appeals has already acted [to stay the District Court's injunction] and the consequence of the order of Mr. Justice DOUGLAS is to set aside the Court of Appeals order.

The consequence of the Court of Appeals' stay order of August 1, 1973, was to preserve the status quo until it could act on the merits. The Court of Appeals, having originally expedited a hearing on the merits to August 13, 1973, has since further expedited the hearing on the merits to August 8, 1973.

Now therefore, the order of the District Court dated July 25, 1973, is hereby stayed pending further order by this Court.

I have been in communication with the other Members of the Court, and . . . CHIEF JUSTICE [BURGER], Mr. Justice BRENNAN, Mr. Justice STEWART, Mr. Justice WHITE, Mr. Justice BLACKMUN, Mr. Justice POWELL, and Mr. Justice REHNQUIST agree with this action.

Justice DOUGLAS dissenting:

The order I entered on August 3, 1973, in *Holtzman v. Schlesinger* not only vacated the stay of the Court of Appeals but also reinstated the judgment of the District Court. I mailed it on August 3, 1973, and reported its contents to the Clerk's office. . . .

My Brother MARSHALL in his opinion of August 4, 1973, misstates the facts when he says that "the only order extant in this case is the order of the District Court." A correct statement would be that the most recent order in this case was my order of August 3, 1973, reinstating the order of the District Court, which would leave the Court of Appeals free to act on the merits and give full relief or, alternatively, permit this Court to reverse me. Under my Brother MARSHALL's order of August 4, 1973, only this Court can act to give injunctive relief.

The Court has unquestioned power to reverse me; and although I disagree with the Court's action on the merits, that is not the point of this dissent. If we who impose law and order are ourselves to be bound by law and order, we can act as a Court only when at least six of us are present.

That is the requirement of the Act of Congress [which says "any six [justices] shall constitute a quorum"]. . . . Seriatim telephone calls cannot, with all respect, be a lawful substitute. A Conference brings us all together; views are exchanged; briefs are studied; oral argument by counsel for each side is customarily required. But even without participation the Court always acts in Conference and therefore responsibly.

Those of the Brethren out of Washington, D.C., on August 4, 1973, could not possibly have studied my opinion in this case. For, although I wrote it late on August 3, it was not released until 9:30 a.m. on August 4; and before 3 p.m., August 4, I was advised by telephone that eight Members of the Court disagreed with me. The issue tendered in the case was not frivolous; the Government on oral argument conceded as much. It involved a new point of law never yet resolved by the Court. I have participated for enough years in Conferences to realize that profound changes are made among the Brethren once their minds are allowed to explore a problem in depth. Yet there were only a few of the Brethren who saw my opinion before they took contrary action.

Whatever may be said on the merits, I am firmly convinced that the telephone disposition of this grave and crucial constitutional issue is not permissible. . . . The principles are that the Court is a deliberative body that acts only on reasoned bases after full consideration, ... A Gallup Poll type of inquiry of widely scattered Justices is, I think, a subversion of the regime under which I thought we lived. . . .

Under the law as it is written, the order of Mr. Justice MARSHALL of August 4, 1973, will in time be reversed by that Higher Court which invariably sits in judgment on the decisions of this Court. . . .

STUMP v. SPARKMAN

435 U.S. 349 (1978)

Justice WHITE delivered the opinion of the Court [joined by Chief Justice BURGER, Justice BLACKMUN, Justice REHNQUIST, and Justice STEVENS. Justice BRENNAN did not participate]:

This case requires us to consider the scope of a judge's immunity from damages liability. . . .

I

The relevant facts underlying the respondents' suit are not in dispute. On July 9, 1971, Ora Spitler McFarlin, the mother of respondent Linda Kay Spitler Sparkman, presented to Judge Harold D. Stump of the Circuit Court of DeKalb County, Ind., a document captioned "Petition to Have

Tubal Ligation Performed on Minor and Indemnity Agreement." The document had been drafted by her attorney, a petitioner here. In this petition, Mrs. McFarlin stated under oath that her daughter was 15 years of age and was "somewhat retarded," although she had attended public school and had been promoted each year with her class. The petition further stated that Linda had been associating with "older youth or young men" and had stayed out overnight with them on several occasions. As a result of this behavior and Linda's mental capabilities, it was stated that it would be in the daughter's best interest if she underwent a tubal ligation in order "to prevent unfortunate circumstances. . . ." In the same document Mrs. McFarlin also undertook to indemnify and hold harmless Dr. John Hines, who was to perform the operation, and the DeKalb Memorial Hospital, where the operation was to take place, against all causes of action that might arise as a result of the performance of the tubal ligation.

The petition was approved by Judge Stump on the same day. He affixed his signature as "Judge, DeKalb Circuit Court," to approve the statement that he did "hereby approve the above Petition. . . ."

On July 15, 1971, Linda Spitler entered the DeKalb Memorial Hospital, having been told that she was to have her appendix removed. The following day a tubal ligation was performed on her. She was released several days later, unaware of the true nature of the surgery.

Approximately two years after the operation, Linda Spitler was married to respondent Leo Sparkman. Her inability to become pregnant led her to discover that she had been sterilized during the 1971 operation. As a result of this revelation, the Sparkmans filed suit . . . against Mrs. McFarlin, her attorney, Judge Stump, the doctors . . . and [the hospital]. Respondents sought damages for alleged violation of Linda Sparkman's constitutional rights; also asserted were pendent state claims for assault and battery, medical malpractice, and loss of potential fatherhood.

. . . The District Court, however, held that no federal action would lie against any of the defendants because Judge Stump, the only state agent, was absolutely immune from suit under the doctrine of judicial immunity. . . .

. . . [T]he Court of Appeals . . . reversed, . . . holding that [the judge had not acted within his jurisdiction]. . . . The Court of Appeals also held that the judge had forfeited his immunity "because of his failure to comply with elementary principles of procedural due process." . . .

. . . We reverse.

II

The governing principle of law is well established and is not questioned by the parties. As early as 1872, the Court recognized that it was "a general principle of the highest importance to the proper administration of justice that a judicial officer, in exercising the authority vested in him, [should] be free to act upon his own convictions without apprehension of personal consequences to himself." . . .

The Court of Appeals correctly recognized that the necessary inquiry in determining whether a defendant judge is immune from suit is whether at the time he took the challenged action he had jurisdiction over the subject matter before him. . . . [T]he scope of the judge's jurisdiction must be construed broadly where the issue is the immunity of the judge. A judge will not be deprived of immunity because the action he took was in error, was done maliciously, or was in excess of his authority; rather he will be subject to liability only when he has acted in the "clear absence of all jurisdiction." . . .

We cannot agree that there was a "clear absence of all jurisdiction" in the DeKalb County Circuit Court to consider the petition presented by Mrs. McFarlin. . . .

. . . A judge is absolutely immune from liability for his judicial acts even if his exercise of authority is flawed by the commission of grave procedural errors. . . .

. . . [Respondents] argue that Judge Stump's approval of the petition was not a judicial act because the petition was not given a docket number, was not placed on file with the clerk's office, and was approved in an *ex parte* proceeding without notice to [Linda Spitler Sparkman], without a hearing, and without the appointment of a *guardian ad litem* [advocate for the minor child]. . . .

The relevant cases demonstrate that the factors determining whether an act by a judge is a "judicial" one relate to the nature of the act itself, *i.e.*, whether it is a function normally performed by a judge, and to the expectations of the parties, *i.e.*, whether they dealt with the judge in his judicial capacity. Here, both factors indicate that Judge Stump's approval of the sterilization was a judicial act. State judges with general jurisdiction not infrequently are called upon in their official capacity to approve petitions relating to the affairs of minors, as for example, a petition to settle a minor's claim. . . .

Both the Court of Appeals and the respondents seem to suggest that, because of the tragic consequences of Judge Stump's actions, he should not be immune. . . . Despite the unfairness to litigants that sometimes results, the doctrine of judicial immunity is thought to be in the best interests of "the proper administration of justice . . . [for it allows] a judicial officer, in exercising the authority vested in him [to] be free to act upon his own convictions, without apprehension of personal consequences to himself." *Bradley v. Fisher* [1872]. . . .

. . . [Judge Stump] is, therefore, under the controlling cases, immune from damages liability even if his approval of the petition was in error. . . .

Justice STEWART dissenting [joined by Justices MARSHALL and POWELL]:

. . . [T]he scope of judicial immunity is limited to liability for "judicial acts," and I think that what Judge Stump did on July 9, 1971, was beyond the pale of anything that could sensibly be called a judicial act. . . .

. . . In Indiana, as elsewhere in our country, a parent is authorized to arrange for and consent to medical and surgical treatment for his minor child. . . . And when a parent decides to call a physician to care for his sick child or arranges to have a surgeon remove his child's tonsils, he does not, "normally" or otherwise, need to seek the approval of a judge. On the other hand, Indiana did in 1971 have statutory procedures for the sterilization of certain people who were *institutionalized.* But these statutes provided for *administrative proceedings* before a board established by the superintendent of each public hospital. Only if after notice and an evidentiary hearing, an order of sterilization was entered in these proceedings could there be review in a circuit court. . . .

In sum, what Judge Stump did on July 9, 1971, was in no way an act "normally performed by a judge." Indeed, there is no reason to believe that such an act has ever been performed by *any* other Indiana judge, either before or since.

. . . There was no "case," controversial or otherwise. There were no litigants. There was and could be no appeal. And there was not even the pretext of principled decision making. The total absence of *any* of these normal attributes of a judicial proceeding convinces me that the conduct complained of in this case was not a judicial act.

The petitioners' brief speaks of an "aura of deism which surrounds the bench . . . essential to the maintenance of respect for the judicial institution." Though the rhetoric may be overblown, I do not quarrel with it. But if aura there be, it is hardly protected by exonerating from liability such lawless conduct as took place here. And if intimidation [of the judiciary through the threat of lawsuits] would serve to deter its recurrence, that would surely be in the public interest.

SPALLONE v. UNITED STATES

110 S. Ct. 625 (1990)

Chief Justice REHNQUIST delivered the opinion of the Court [joined by Justices WHITE, O'CONNOR, SCALIA, and KENNEDY]:

This case is the most recent episode of a lengthy lawsuit in which the city of Yonkers was held liable for intentionally enhancing racial segregation in housing in Yonkers. The issue here is whether it was a proper exercise of judicial power for the District Court to hold petitioners, four Yonkers councilmembers, in contempt for refusing to vote in favor of legislation implementing a consent decree earlier approved by the city. We hold that in the circumstances of this case the District Court abused its discretion.

I

In 1980, the United States filed a complaint alleging, *inter alia*, that the two named defendants—the city of Yonkers and the Yonkers Community Development Agency—had intentionally engaged in a pattern and practice of housing discrimination. . . .

The District Court found the two named defendants liable, concluding that the segregative effect of the city's actions had been "consistent and extreme," and that "the desire to preserve existing patterns of segregation ha[d] been a significant factor in the sustained community opposition to subsidized housing in East Yonkers and other overwhelmingly white areas of the City." . . . [P]arts of the remedial order were directed only to the city. They required affirmative steps to disperse public housing throughout Yonkers. . . . The court did not mandate specific details of the plan such as how many subsidized units must be developed, where they should be constructed, or how the city should provide for the units. . . .

. . . [I]n January 1988, the parties agreed to a consent decree that set forth "certain actions which the City of Yonkers [would] take in connection with a consensual implementation" . . . of the housing remedy order. . . . The decree was approved by the city council in a 5-to-2 vote (petitioners Spallone and Chema voting no). . . .

For several more months, however, the city continued to delay action toward implementing the long-term [remedial] plan. . . . As a result of the city's intransigence, the United States and the NAACP moved the court for the entry of a Long Term Plan Order based on a draft that had been prepared by the city's lawyers during negotiations. . . . After several weeks of further delay the court, after a hearing held on July 26, 1988, entered an order requiring the city of Yonkers to enact on or before August 1, 1988, the "legislative package" described in a section of the earlier consent decree; . . . .

Further provisions of the order specified escalating daily amounts of fines in the event of contempt, and providing that if the legislation were not enacted before August 10, 1988, any councilmember who remained in contempt should be committed to the custody of the United States

Marshal for imprisonment. The specific daily fines for the city were $100 for the first day, to be doubled for each consecutive day of noncompliance; the specified daily fine for members of the city council was $500 per day.

Notwithstanding the threat of substantial sanctions, on August 1 the city council defeated a resolution of intent to adopt the legislative package . . . by a vote of 4 to 3 (petitioners constituting the majority). On August 2, the District court held a hearing to afford the city and the councilmembers an opportunity to show cause why they should not be adjudicated in contempt. It rejected the city's arguments, held the city in contempt, and imposed the coercive sanctions set forth in the July 26 order. After questioning the individual council members as to the reasons for their negative votes, the court also held each of the petitioners in contempt and imposed sanctions. . . .

With the city's daily contempt sanction approaching $1 million per day, the city council finally enacted the Affordable Housing Ordinance on September 9, 1988, by a vote of 5 to 2, petitioners Spallone and Fagan voting no. Because the contempt orders raise important issues about the appropriate exercise of the federal judicial power against individual legislators, we granted certiorari. . . .

II

The issue before us is relatively narrow. There can be no question about the liability of the city of Yonkers for racial discrimination. . . . Nor do we have before us any question as to the District Court's remedial order. . . . Our focus, then, is only on the District Court's order of July 26 imposing contempt sanctions on the individual petitioners if they failed to vote in favor of the ordinance in question. . . .

In selecting a means to enforce the consent judgment, the District Court was entitled to rely on the axiom that "courts have inherent power to enforce compliance with their lawful orders through civil contempt." . . . When a district court's order is necessary to remedy past discrimination, the court has an additional basis for the exercise of broad equitable powers. . . . But while "remedial powers of an equity court must be adequate to the task, . . . they are not unlimited." . . . "[T]he federal courts in devising a remedy must take into account the interests of state and local authorities in managing their own affairs, consistent with the Constitution." . . .

Given that the city had entered a consent judgment committing itself to enact legislation implementing the long-term plan, we certainly cannot say it was an abuse of discretion for the District Court to have chosen contempt sanctions against the city, as opposed to petitioners, as a means of ensuring compliance. . . . Petitioners, the individual city councilmen, on the other hand, were not parties to the action, and they had not been found individually liable for any of the violations upon which the remedial decree was based. . . .

The nub of the matter, then, is whether in the light of the reasonable probability that sanctions against the city would accomplish the desired result, it was within the court's discretion to impose sanctions on the petitioners as well under the circumstances of this case. . . .

Sanctions directed against the city for failure to take actions such as required by the consent decree coerce the city legislators and, of course, restrict the freedom of those legislators to act in accordance with their current views of the city's best interest. But we believe there are significant differences between the two types of fines. The imposition of sanctions on individual legislators is designed to cause them to vote, not with a view to the interest of their constituents or of the city, but with a view solely to their own personal interests. . . . Such fines thus encourage legislators, in effect, to declare that they favor an ordinance not in order to avoid bankrupting the city for which they legislate, but in order to avoid bankrupting themselves.

This sort of individual sanction effects a much greater perversion of the normal legislative process than does the imposition of sanctions on the city. . . . In that case, the legislator is only encouraged to vote in favor of an ordinance that he would not otherwise favor by reason of the adverse sanctions imposed on the city. A councilman who felt that his constituents would rather have the city enact the Affordable Housing Ordinance than pay a "bankrupting fine" would be motivated to vote in favor of such an ordinance because the sanctions were a threat to the fiscal solvency of the city for whose welfare he was in part responsible. This is the sort of calculus in which legislators engage regularly.

We hold that the District Court, in view of the "extraordinary" nature of the imposition of sanctions against the individual councilmen, should have proceeded with such contempt sanctions first against the city alone in order to secure compliance with remedial orders. Only if that approach failed to produce compliance within a reasonable time should the question of imposing contempt sanctions against petitioners have been considered. . . .

Justice BRENNAN dissenting [joined by Justices MARSHALL, BLACK-MUN, and STEVENS]:

. . . We must all hope that no court will ever again face the open and sustained official defiance of established constitutional values and valid judicial orders that prompted Judge Sand's invocation of the contempt power in this manner. But I firmly believe that its availability for such use, in extreme circumstances, is essential. . . .

I cannot accept this parsimonious view of the District Court's discretion to wield the power of contempt. Judge Sand's intimate contact for many years with the recalcitrant councilmembers and his familiarity with the city's political climate gave him special insight into the best way to coerce compliance when all cooperative efforts failed. From our detached vantage point, we can hardly judge as well as he which coercive sanctions or combination thereof were most likely to work quickly and least disruptively. . . .

II

. . . Although the escalating city fines eventually would have seriously disrupted many public services and employment, . . . the Court's failure even to consider the possibility that the councilmembers would maintain their defiant posture despite the threat of fiscal insolvency bespeaks an ignorance of Yonkers' history of entrenched discrimination and an indifference to Yonkers' political reality.

The Court first fails to adhere today to our longstanding recognition that the "district court has firsthand experience with the parties and is best qualified to deal with the 'flinty, intractable realities of day-to-day implementation of constitutional commands.' " . . . Deference to the [district] court's exercise of discretion is particularly appropriate where, as here, the record clearly reveals that the court employed extreme caution before taking the final step of holding the councilmembers personally in contempt. Judge Sand patiently weathered a whirlwind of evasive maneuvers and misrepresentations; . . . considered and rejected alternative means of securing compliance other than contempt sanctions; and carefully considered the ramifications of personal fines. . . .

As the events leading up to the Contempt Order make clear, the recalcitrant councilmembers were extremely responsive to the strong segments of their constituencies that were vociferously opposed to racial residential integration. . . .

. . . [I]t seems to me entirely appropriate—indeed obligatory—for Judge Sand to have considered, not just whether city sanctions alone would *eventually* have coerced compliance, but also *how promptly* they would have done so. . . .

I concede that personal sanctions against legislators intuitively may seem less appropriate than more traditional forms of coercing compliance with court orders. But this intuition does not withstand close scrutiny given the circumstances of this case. When necessary, courts levy personal contempt sanctions against other types of state and local officials for flouting valid court orders, and I see no reason to treat local legislators differently when they are acting outside of their "sphere of legitimate legislative activity." . . .

III

The Court's decision today that Judge Sand abused his remedial discretion by imposing personal fines simultaneously with city fines creates no new principle of law; indeed, it invokes no principle of any sort. But it directs a message to district judges that, despite their repeated and close contact with the various parties and issues, even the most delicate remedial choices by the most conscientious and deliberate judges are subject to being second-guessed by this Court. I hope such a message will not daunt the courage of district courts who, if ever again faced with such protracted defiance, must carefully yet firmly secure compliance with their remedial orders. But I worry that the Court's message will have the unintended effect of emboldening recalcitrant officials continually to test the ultimate reach of the remedial authority of the federal courts, thereby postponing the day when all public officers finally accept that "the responsibility of those who exercise power in a democratic government is not to reflect inflamed public feeling but to help form its understanding." . . .

MISSOURI v. JENKINS

110 S. Ct. 1651 (1990)

Justice WHITE delivered the opinion of the Court [joined by Justices BRENNAN, MARSHALL, BLACKMUN, and STEVENS]:

The United States District Court for the Western District of Missouri imposed an increase in property taxes levied by the Kansas City, Missouri, School District (KCMSD) to ensure funding for the desegregation of KCMSD's public schools. . . .

I

. . . [In 1984] [a]fter a lengthy trial, the District Court found that KCMSD and the State [of Missouri] operated a segregated school system within the KCMSD. . . .

The District Court thereafter issued an order detailing the remedies necessary to eliminate the vestiges of segregation and the financing necessary to implement those remedies. . . . The Missouri Constitution limits local property taxes to $1.25 per $100 of assessed valuation unless a majority of the voters in the district approve a higher levy, up to $3.25 per $100; the levy may be raised above $3.25 per $100 only if two-thirds of the voters agree. . . .

. . . The District Court concluded that it would be "clearly inequitable" to require the population of KCMSD to pay half of the desegregation cost, and that "even with Court help it would be very difficult for the KCMSD to fund more than 25% of the costs of the entire remedial plan." . . . The court reasoned that the State should pay for most of the desegregation cost under the principle that " 'the person who starts the fire has more responsibility for the damages caused than the person who fails to put it out,' " . . . and that apportionment of damages between the State and KCMSD according to fault was supported by the doctrine of comparative fault in tort. . . . The District Court then held that the State and KCMSD were 75% and 25% at fault, respectively, and ordered them to share the cost of the desegregation remedy in that proportion. . . .

Three months later . . . it was clear that KCMSD would lack the resources to pay for its 25% share of the desegregation cost. . . . Finding itself with "no choice but to exercise its broad equitable powers and enter a judgment that will enable KCMSD to raise its share of the cost of the plan," . . . and believing that the "United States Supreme Court has stated that a tax may be increased if 'necessary to raise funds adequate to . . . operate and maintain without racial discrimination a public school system,' " . . . the court ordered the KCMSD property tax levy raised from $2.05 to $4.00 per $100 of assessed valuation through the 1991–1992 fiscal year. . . .

III

We turn to the tax increase imposed by the District Court. The State urges us to hold that the tax increase violated Article III, the Tenth Amendment, and principles of federal/state comity. We find it unnecessary to reach the difficult constitutional issues, for we agree with the State that the tax increase contravened the principles of comity that must govern the exercise of the District Court's equitable discretion in this area.

It is accepted by all the parties, as it was by the courts below, that the imposition of a tax increase by a federal court was an extraordinary event. . . . Before taking such a drastic step the District Court was obliged to assure itself that no permissible alternative would have accomplished the required task. . . .

The District Court believed that it had no alternative to imposing a tax increase. But there was an alternative, the very one outlined by the Court of Appeals: it could have authorized or required the KCMSD to levy property taxes at a rate adequate to fund the desegregation remedy and could have enjoined the operation of state laws that would have prevented KCMSD from exercising this power. . . . The difference between the two approaches is far more than a matter of form. Authorizing and directing local government institutions to devise and implement remedies not only protects the function of those institutions but, to the extent possible, also places the responsibility for solutions to the problems of segregation upon those who have themselves created the problems. . . .

The District Court therefore abused its discretion in imposing the tax itself. . . .

IV

. . . .

The State maintains, however, that even under these cases, the federal judicial power can go no further than to require local governments to levy taxes *as authorized under state law.* In other words, the State argues that federal courts cannot set aside state-imposed limitations on local taxing authority because to do so is to do more than to require the local government "to exercise the power *that is theirs."* We disagree. . . .

It is therefore clear that a local government with taxing authority may be ordered to levy taxes in excess of the limit set by state statute where there is reason based in the Constitution for not observing the statutory limitation. . . . Here the KCMSD may be ordered to levy taxes despite the statutory limitations on its authority in order to compel discharge of an obligation imposed on KCMSD by the Fourteenth Amendment['s Equal Protection Clause]. To hold otherwise would fail to take account of the obligations of local governments, under the Supremacy Clause, to fulfill the requirements that the Constitution imposes on them. However wide the discretion of local authorities in fashioning desegregation remedies may be, "if a state-imposed limitation on a school authority's discretion operates to inhibit or obstruct the operation of a unitary school system or impede the disestablishing of a dual school system, it must fall; state policy must give way when it operates to hinder vindication of federal constitutional guarantees." . . . Even though a particular remedy may not be required in every case to vindicate constitutional guarantees, where (as here) it has been found that a particular remedy is required, the State cannot hinder the process by preventing a local government from implementing that remedy. . . .

Justice KENNEDY concurring in part [joined by Chief Justice REHNQUIST and Justices O'CONNOR and SCALIA]:

. . . .

In my view, however, the Court transgresses [important] principles when it goes further, much further, to embrace by broad dictum an expansion of power in the federal judiciary beyond all precedent. Today's casual embrace of taxation imposed by the unelected, life-tenured federal judiciary disregards fundamental precepts for the democratic control of public institutions. . . .

I

. . . .

The judicial taxation approved by the Eighth Circuit is also without parallel. Other Circuits that have faced funding problems arising from remedial decrees have concluded that, while courts have undoubted power to order that schools operate in compliance with the Constitution, the manner and methods of school financing are beyond federal judicial authority. . . .

The premise of the Court's analysis, I submit, is infirm. Any purported distinction between direct imposition of a tax by the federal court and an order commanding the school district to impose the tax is but a convenient formalism where the court's action is predicated on elimination of state law limitations on the school district's taxing authority. . . .

. . . The Court never confronts the judicial authority to issue an order for this purpose. Absent a change in state law, the tax is imposed by federal authority under a federal decree. The question is whether a district court possesses a power to tax under federal law, either directly or through delegation to the KCMSD.

II

Article III of the Constitution states that "[t]he judicial Power of the United States, shall be vested in one supreme Court, and in such inferior Courts as the Congress may from time to time ordain and establish." The description of the judicial power nowhere includes the word "tax" or anything that resembles it. This reflects the Framers' understanding that taxation was not a proper area for judicial involvement. . . .

The nature of the District Court's order here reveals that it is not a proper exercise of the judicial power. The exercise of judicial power involves adjudication of controversies and imposition of burdens on those who are parties before the Court. The order at issue here is not of this character. It binds the broad class of all KCMSD taxpayers. It has the purpose and direct effect of extracting money from persons who had no presence or representation in the suit. For this reason, the District Court's direct order imposing a tax was more than an abuse of discretion, for any attempt to collect the taxes from the citizens would have been a blatant denial of due process. . . .

A judicial taxation order is but an attempt to exercise a power that always has been thought legislative in nature. . . .

The power of taxation is one that the federal judiciary does not possess. In our system "the legislative department alone has access to the pockets of the people," . . . for it is the legislature that is accountable to them and represents their will. . . .

III

. . . .

The District Court here did consider alternatives to the taxing measures it imposed, but only *funding* alternatives. . . . There is no indication in the record that the District Court gave any consideration to the possibility that an alternative remedial plan, while less attractive from an educational policy viewpoint, might nonetheless suffice to cure the constitutional violation. Rather, it found only that the taxation orders were necessary to fund the particular remedy it had devised. This Court, with full justification, has given latitude to the district judges that must deal with persisting problems of desegregation. Even when faced with open defiance of the mandate of educational equality, however, no court has ever found necessary a remedy of the scope presented here. For this reason, no order of taxation has ever been approved. The Court fails to provide any explanation why this case presents the need to endorse by dictum so drastic a step. . . .

IV

This case is a stark illustration of the ever-present question whether ends justify means. Few ends are more important than enforcing the guarantee of equal educational opportunity for our Nation's children. But rules of taxation that override state political structures not themselves subject to any constitutional infirmity raise serious questions of federal authority, questions compounded by the odd posture of a case in which the Court assumes the validity of a novel conception of desegregation remedies we never before have approved. The historical record of voluntary compliance with the decree of *Brown v. Board of Education* is not a proud chapter in our constitutional history, and the judges of the District Courts and Courts of Appeals have been courageous and skillful in implementing its mandate. But courage and skill must be exercised with due regard for the proper and historic role of the courts.

... Indeed, while this case happens to arise in the compelling context of school desegregation, the principles involved are not limited to that context. There is no obvious limit to today's discussion that would prevent judicial taxation cases involving prisons, hospitals, or other public institutions. ... This assertion of judicial power in one of the most sensitive of policy areas, that involving taxation, begins a process that over time could threaten fundamental alteration of the form of government our Constitution embodies.

James Madison observed: "Justice is the end of government. It is the end of civil society. It ever has been, and ever will be pursued, until it be obtained, or until liberty be lost in the pursuit." ... In pursuing the demand of justice for racial equality, I fear that the Court today loses sight of other basic political liberties guaranteed by our constitutional system, liberties that can coexist with a proper exercise of judicial remedial powers adequate to correct constitutional violations.

Questions

1. If the Constitution defines which branch can declare "war" and the Supreme Court is responsible for interpreting the Constitution, why did the Court decline to hear *Mora v. McNamara*?
2. Do the words of the Constitution reserve foreign policy decisions for any particular branch? Do the words of the Constitution preclude the Supreme Court from hearing any issues that require interpretation of the Constitution and federal statutes?
3. In *Holtzman*, Justice Marshall asserts that "[w]e have a government of limited powers, and those limits pertain to the Justices of this Court." What limitations apply to the powers of the Supreme Court? How can we identify the limitations that apply?
4. Is Justice Douglas correct in claiming that the issue in *Holtzman* is analogous to a death penalty case?
5. Did the Supreme Court utilize proper judicial procedures in overruling Justice Douglas?
6. What would have happened if the Supreme Court had ordered the Nixon Administration to stop bombing Cambodia?
7. What "Higher Court" was Justice Douglas referring to in *Schlesinger v. Holtzman* when he said that the Supreme Court's order would ultimately be reversed? Public opinion? History? "God"? Or was it merely dramatic rhetoric?

8. Would society be harmed if the Supreme Court permitted the judge to be sued in *Stump v. Sparkman*?

9. What is the difference between a judge acting "in excess of his [or her] authority," in which case the judge may not be sued, or acting in "clear absence of all jurisdiction," which would permit the imposition of liability? Who would decide which classification applies?

10. Has the Supreme Court given the judiciary excessive protection from civil liability? Does this level of protection make judges even less accountable to the public?

11. In *Spallone v. United States* and *Missouri v. Jenkins*, the Supreme Court limits the ability of district judges to enforce court orders. Do these cases establish any principles or definable limitations that will restrain federal judges in future cases?

12. After the decision in *Spallone*, how difficult will it be for a district judge to fine individual local officials for noncompliance with court orders?

13. After the decision in *Missouri*, how difficult will it be for a district judge to ensure that property taxes are raised to pay for remedial measures in a school desegregation case?

14. Is Justice Kennedy correct that the Court's distinctions in *Missouri* are "but a convenient formalism" and that judges are effectively empowered to raise taxes so long as they do not order the tax levy directly? If so, why did the majority bother to overrule the district judge if the judge is permitted to attain the same end (i.e., raising taxes) through another means? Does *Spallone* present an analogous situation?

15. In his concluding paragraph in *Missouri*, Justice Kennedy implies that there are alternative remedies that are "adequate to correct constitutional violations." In the Kansas City case, what would be examples of these effective alternatives? Why are there no specific examples of these alternatives listed in Kennedy's opinion?

16. Will the *Spallone* decision fulfill Justice Brennan's fears that local officials will feel encouraged to resist judicial orders? If so, what will the Supreme Court do?

17. Will the *Missouri* decision encourage judges to seek tax increases in order to redress constitutional problems in prisons (e.g., overcrowded conditions) and other public institutions? If not, why not?

18. Although the Supreme Court acknowledged that there were competing arguments in all three cases, did the Court adequately consider and balance all of the important societal and legal interests in presenting the decisions in *Stump*, *Spallone*, and *Missouri*? Has the "balance of power" among the branches of government changed as a result of these opinions?

FOUR

Judicial Interpretation
in Historical Context

The attitudes and values of human beings, including the justices of the Supreme Court, are shaped by the historical settings in which they are socialized and educated. Justices of the Supreme Court usually espouse the prevailing values of their era. Archibald Cox explained, for example, that historical forces affected the decisions of the conservative justices who blocked legislative initiatives on economic and social welfare policies in the early twentieth century:

> All of the Supreme Court justices who participated in the consideration of *Lochner v. New York* were born in the 1830s and 1840s. They grew up in an America ignorant of large-scale industrial organization, urban squalor, and the helplessness of the individual in dealing with organized wealth. The ideas they expressed were not unsuited to their early years [when the United States was an agrarian society]. Probably most law must lag slightly behind the march of change.[1]

There are many examples of Supreme Court decisions that reflect the influences of accepted beliefs during particular historical eras. The justices manifested the prevailing nineteenth-century views about the proper place of women in society when, in *Bradwell v. Illinois* (1873), they said that women could be barred from becoming attorneys because "[t]he natural and proper timidity and delicacy which belongs to the female sex evidently unfits it for many . . . occupations." In *Plessy v. Ferguson* (1896), the justices endorsed racial segregation because they took for

1. Archibald Cox, *The Court and the Constitution* (Boston: Houghton Mifflin, 1987), p. 136.

granted that racial groups possessed innate differences and would naturally prefer to have separate facilities.

As members of American society, the justices are influenced by the historical events and trends that shape the rest of society. The Supreme Court's endorsement, in *Korematsu v. United States* (1944), of the relocation and incarceration of Japanese-Americans during World War II is attributable to the justices' fears and concerns about how the United States was faring in its war against Japan. The infamous decision is not easily explainable according to any words contained in the Constitution.

Although the justices of the Supreme Court generally follow the prevailing views of their era, there are moments when they may help to lead evolutionary changes in American society. In *Brown v. Board of Education* (1954), the Supreme Court stepped ahead of society in issuing its monumental symbolic declaration about racial equality. The decision did not lead to an instantaneous transformation of American society; it did not even lead to the desegregation of all American school systems. Schools throughout the country had ample opportunity to resist the decision, and incomplete reforms were implemented over the course of several decades on a city-by-city basis (*see Missouri v. Jenkins*, 1990, reprinted in chapter 3). The Court's decision in *Brown* did, however, through its symbolic value, push other government institutions toward fulfilling the constitutional goals of "equal protection" and provide encouragement for growing political activisim in the pursuit of civil rights.

The push for reform provided by the Supreme Court in the 1950s did not yield strong results in Congress until the 1960s, after receiving additional impetus from the civil rights movement, from reactions to President Kennedy's assassination, and from President Johnson's legislative skills. One portion of the Civil Rights Act of 1964, specifically Title II, attacked racial discrimination in the provision of public accommodations (e.g., hotels, motels, restaurants, etc.). In 1875, after the Civil War, Congress had passed similar laws against racial discrimination. The Supreme Court, however, reflecting both the justices' interpretation of the intent of the Fourteenth Amendment and their era's relaxed attitudes about the harms of racial discrimination, invalidated legislative efforts to prevent discrimination by private businesses (*Civil Rights Cases*, 1883). In the 1960s, the Supreme Court faced the identical issue once again. Could Congress forbid discrimination by private businesses? The relevant words of the Constitution had not changed since the previous decision on the issue, but the political and social environment of American society had changed significantly by the 1960s.

The fundamental legal problem was that congressional authority to pass legislation enforcing the Equal Protection Clause appeared limited by the Fourteenth Amendment's declaration that "No *state* shall . . . deny to any person . . . equal protection of the laws" (emphasis added). The Constitution's words did not expressly empower Congress to attack private discrimination that clashes with equal protection values. In 1883, the Supreme Court focused upon this precise language to conclude that Congress lacked the power to regulate such private conduct. In the 1960s, Congress sought to avoid this issue by asserting its authority to attack private discrimination through its constitutional power to regulate interstate commerce. After asserting this new approach, Congress had to wait to see whether the twentieth-century Supreme Court would approve this novel utilization of the Commerce Clause to redress racial discrimination.

In the cases and legislative testimony reprinted in this chapter, the justices demonstrated that they were part of a new era in American history. In approving the congressional legislation, they were not leading the country as they had done in *Brown* during the previous decade. Instead, they reverted to their more usual role of endorsing and providing legitimacy for new initiatives by the other branches of government. As Robert Dahl observed, the Supreme Court's function for most of American history has been "to confer legality and constitutionality on the fundamental policies of the successful [political] coalition [that controls the institutions of government]."[2] The Supreme Court's endorsement of antidiscrimination laws brought the judiciary together with the other branches of government in a new unified stand against racial discrimination. Although the Court's decisions both reflected and contributed to the historical evolution of American society toward equality, as the following cases and questions indicate, its interpretation of the Commerce Clause simultaneously created a new set of issues concerning the permissible scope of congressional power.

CIVIL RIGHTS—PUBLIC ACCOMMODATIONS, HEARINGS BEFORE THE U.S. SENATE, COMMITTEE ON COMMERCE, WASHINGTON, D.C., JULY 1, 1963.

ROBERT F. KENNEDY, ATTORNEY GENERAL OF THE UNITED STATES

So I think it only fair, Mr. Chairman, to declare that this bill does not seriously or significantly interfere with private property rights nor does

---

2. Robert A. Dahl, *Democracy in the United States: Promise and Performance*, 4th ed. (Boston, MA: Houghton Mifflin, 1981), p. 161.

it extend any principle of Federal regulation. Therefore, the argument should be rejected as a smokescreen. The real issue is whether Congress should or should not ban racial discrimination in places open to the public. . . .

It seems to me beyond question that every provision of this bill is a legitimate exercise of Congress' authority over interstate commerce.

In addition to the commerce clause, we rely on Congress' power under the 14th amendment, to prohibit the denial of equal protection laws to any person. . . .

We recognize that in 1883 the Supreme Court held in the *Civil Rights Cases* (109 U.S.3), Congress did not have power under the 14th amendment to prohibit discrimination in privately owned places of public accommodation, and that Congress' power under that amendment is only over discrimination accomplished by the action of a State. . . .

There are a number of recent cases in which the Federal courts have held that private decisions that discriminate may be attributed to the State for purposes of the 14th amendment. Consequently, if the Supreme Court were now asked to pass upon the constitutionality of a public accommodations law based on the 14th amendment, it might well uphold the law.

However, the 1883 decision has not been overruled and remains the law of the land. It is for this reason that we rely primarily on the commerce clause.

Some Congressmen, who seek objectives similar to those of this bill, would place sole reliance on the 14th amendment. There are others who strongly oppose any reliance on the 14th amendment.

We recognize that there is some merit in both positions. However, we feel it is absolutely clear that Congress has the power to end discrimination in places of public accommodation under the provisions of the commerce clause. Should it ultimately be decided that Congress can regulate these businesses under the 14th amendment, the fact that the bill describes them in terms of their impact on interstate commerce, would not diminish Congress' power.

Virtually all people in the public accommodations business will know if they are covered by this bill. . . .

Restaurants and retail stores are covered if a substantial part of their business is with interstate travelers; or if a substantial part of their wares has moved in interstate commerce; or if their activities substantially affect interstate commerce; or if they are an integral part of another business covered by any of these other provisions.

The significant question in these definitions is, What is meant by "substantial" or "substantially"? While the meaning of those words cannot be reduced to mathematical precision, our intention is that they mean something more than minimal. . . . [I]n the great majority of cases, coverage will be plain. . . .

[W]e didn't want to interfere with somebody's social life. I don't think Congress has the authority under the Constitution, or in any other way, to pass laws that deal with one's social relationships. . . .

If a person is a small person, and wants to discriminate . . . he must actively want to discriminate. If he doesn't know whether he is covered, he can take it to the court and ultimately the worst that can happen to him is that he must stop discriminating. We don't think that is a terribly heavy burden. . . .

SENATOR STROM THURMOND [of South Carolina]: In simple words, the people of the country did not favor the 18th amendment [regarding the prohibition of alcohol] which is an attempt to dictate morals, public opinion rose up and it was repealed. Do you think that this bill here, if public opinion rises up would have the same effect?

MR. KENNEDY: I think I have answered that question. I think it has an effect on the economy at the present time and I think that this bill if it is passed would be supported by the vast majority of Americans. . . .

SEN. THURMOND: Now how could the denial of services to an individual who is a resident and has no intention of leaving that State be a burden on interstate commerce?

MR. KENNEDY: Because we are talking about a cumulative situation here, Senator. It is not just an individual. If this was just an individual situation and there was one restaurant or one motel or one hotel, we wouldn't all be sitting here today.

What this is is a general practice, and a practice that has existed for many, many, many years. What we are trying to do is to get at that.

The cumulative effect of a number of establishments which take in transients, and some of which would be interstate, some of which would be intrastate—the cumulative effect of all these has a major effect on interstate commerce. That is the theory, and it is a theory that has been borne out in a number of decisions. And I suppose the best known is *Wickard v. Filburn*, where the man just ran his own wheat farm. . . .

SEN. THURMOND: Suppose a barbershop got half the business from out-of-state travelers. . . .

MR. KENNEDY: I think it would be covered.

SEN. THURMOND: What about 40 percent?

MR. KENNEDY: I think it would probably be covered.

SEN. THURMOND: What about 30 percent?

MR. KENNEDY: I think you are getting close now, Senator. I think it depends. Where is this barbershop? . . .

SEN. THURMOND: Well, say a fellow got only one out of five, 20 percent of his business from interstate travelers, would that be covered?

MR. KENNEDY: And this fellow wanted to discriminate? . . .

SEN. THURMOND: Suppose he does want to discriminate. Suppose he prefers to cut the hair of only certain people. . . . If only 20 percent of his business is interstate would he have to serve everybody?

MR. KENNEDY: No; he would have to serve—he could not discriminate against anybody because of their race, color, or creed or national origin.

SEN. THURMOND: Twenty percent?

MR. KENNEDY: Again, I think it would depend on other factors.

SEN. THURMOND: What other factors?

MR. KENNEDY: Was he near an airport, Senator? I don't know.

SEN. THURMOND: What difference does it make whether he is near an airport or 10 miles from the airport if 20 percent of his business came from out of State? Would he have to serve them?

MR. KENNEDY: I think these factors play a role in it, Senator—whether an establishment deals with those in interstate commerce. That would be a factor you have to take into consideration. I would say that perhaps it very well might be covered. . . .

SEN. THURMOND: Suppose he wants to serve whom he pleases and [the government] charge[s] him with a violation of this law. He would have to ask [all of his customers] where they live in order to know whether or not. . . .

MR. KENNEDY: Is he a man that wants to discriminate or not, Senator?

SEN. THURMOND: Well, I wouldn't say he wants to discriminate. He just wants to serve whom he pleases.

MR. KENNEDY: Senator, if he doesn't want to discriminate I suppose he could say "I can serve a Negro."

SEN. THURMOND: He just wants to exercise his free American choice. . . .

KATZENBACH v. McCLUNG

379 U.S. 294 (1964)

Justice Clark delivered the opinion of the [unanimous] Court:

. . . .

. . . It is important that a decision on the constitutionality of the Act as applied in these cases be announced as quickly as possible. . . .

2. The Facts.

Ollie's Barbecue is a family-owned restaurant in Birmingham, Alabama, specializing in barbecued meats and homemade pies, with a seating capacity of 220 customers. It is located on a state highway 11 blocks from an interstate one and a somewhat greater distance from railroad and bus stations. The restaurant caters to a family and white-collar trade with a take-out service for Negroes. It employs 36 persons, two-thirds of whom are Negroes.

In the 12 months preceding the passage of the Act, the restaurant purchased approximately $150,000 worth of food, $69,683 or 46% of which was meat it bought from a local supplier who had procured it from outside the State. The District Court expressly found that a substantial portion of the food served in the restaurant had moved in interstate commerce. The restaurant has refused to serve Negroes in its dining accommodations since its original opening in 1927 and since July 2, 1964, it has been operating in violation of the Act. . . .

. . . [T]he [district] court held . . . there was no demonstrable connection between food purchased in interstate commerce and sold in a restaurant and the conclusion of Congress that discrimination in the restaurant would affect commerce. . . .

3. The Act as Applied.

. . . .

. . . The sole question, therefore, narrows down to whether Title II, as applied to a restaurant annually receiving about $70,000 worth of food which has moved in commerce, is a valid exercise of the power of Congress. . . .

4. The Congressional Hearings.

. . . This diminutive spending springing from a refusal to serve Negroes and their total loss as customers has, regardless of the absence of direct evidence, a close connection to interstate commerce. . . .

Moreover, there was an impressive array of testimony that discrimination in restaurants had a direct and highly restrictive effect upon interstate travel by Negroes. This resulted, it was said because discriminatory practices prevent Negroes from buying prepared food served on the premises while on a trip, except in isolated and unkempt restaurants and under most unsatisfactory and often unpleasant conditions. This obviously discourages travel and obstructs interstate commerce for one can hardly travel without eating. Likewise, it was said, that discrimination deterred professional, as well as skilled, people from moving into areas where such practices occurred and thereby caused industry to be reluctant to establish there.

We believe that this testimony afforded ample basis for the conclusion that established restaurants in such areas sold less interstate goods because of the discrimination, that interstate travel was obstructed directly by it, that business in general suffered and that many new businesses refrained from establishing there as a result. Hence the District Court was in error. . . .

It goes without saying that, viewed in isolation, the volume of food purchased by Ollie's Barbecue from sources supplied from out of state was insignificant when compared with the total foodstuffs moving in commerce. But, as our late Brother Jackson said for the Court in *Wickard v. Filburn* . . . (1942):

> "That appellee's own contribution to the demand for wheat may be trivial by itself is not enough to remove him from the scope of federal regulation where, as here, his contribution, taken together with that of many others similarly situated, is far from trivial."

We noted in *Heart of Atlanta Motel* [the companion case on Title II's application to hotels and motels,] that a number of witnesses attested to the fact that racial discrimination was not merely a state or regional problem but was one of nationwide scope. . . .

With the situation spreading as the record shows, Congress was not required to await the total dislocation of commerce. . . .

5. *The Power of Congress to Regulate Local Activities.*

. . . .

Here, . . . Congress has determined for itself that refusals of service to Negroes have imposed burdens both upon the interstate flow of food and upon the movement of products generally. Of course, the mere fact that

Congress has said when particular activity shall be deemed to affect commerce does not preclude further examination by this Court. But where we find that the legislators, in the facts and testimony before them, have a rational basis for finding a chosen regulatory scheme necessary to the protection of commerce, our investigation is at an end. . . .

The absence of direct evidence connecting discriminatory restaurant service with the flow of interstate food, a factor on which the appellees place much reliance, is not, given the evidence as to the effect of such practices on other aspects of commerce, a crucial matter.

The power of Congress in this field is broad and sweeping; where it keeps within its sphere and violates no express constitutional limitation it has been the rule of this court, going back almost to the founding days of the Republic, not to interfere. The Civil Rights Act of 1964, as here applied, we find to be plainly appropriate in the resolution of what the Congress found to be a national commercial problem of the first magnitude. We find it in no violation of any express limitations of the Constitution and we therefore declare it valid. . . .

Justice BLACK concurring [in companion case of *Heart of Atlanta Motel v. United States*, 379 U.S. 241 (1964)]:

. . . .

I

It requires no novel or strained interpretation of the Commerce Clause to sustain Title II as applied in either of these cases [concerning the Heart of Atlanta Motel and Ollie's Barbecue]. . . .

. . . [E]very remote, possible, speculative effect on commerce should not be accepted as an adequate constitutional ground to uproot and throw into the discard all our traditional distinctions between what is purely local, and therefore controlled by state laws, and what affects the national interest and is therefore subject to control by federal laws. I recognize too that some isolated remote lunchroom which sells only to local people and buys almost all its supplies in the locality may possibly be beyond the reach of the power of Congress to regulate commerce, just as such an establishment is not covered by the present Act. But in deciding the constitutional power of Congress in cases like the two before us we do not consider the effect on interstate commerce of only one isolated, individual, local event without regard to the fact that this single local event when added to many others of a similar nature may impose a burden on interstate commerce by reducing its volume or distorting its flow. . . . Measuring, as this Court has so often held is required, by the aggregate effect of a great number of such acts of discrimination, I am of the opinion that the Congress has constitutional power under the Commerce and Necessary and Proper Clauses to protect interstate commerce from the injuries bound to befall it from these discriminatory practices. . . .

Justice DOUGLAS concurring [in *Heart of Atlanta Motel*]:

Though I join the Court's opinions, I am somewhat reluctant here, . . . to rest solely on the Commerce Clause. My reluctance is not due to any conviction that Congress lacks power to regulate commerce in the interest of human rights. It is rather my belief that the right of people to be free of state action that discriminates against them because of race . . . "occupies a more protected position in our constitutional system than does the movement of cattle, fruit, steel and coal across state lines." . . .

Hence I would prefer to rest on the assertion of legislative power contained in [article] 5 of the Fourteenth Amendment. . . .

A decision based on the Fourteenth Amendment would have a more settling effect, making unnecessary litigation over whether a particular restaurant or inn is within the commerce definitions of the Act or whether a particular customer is an interstate traveler. Under my construction, the Act would apply to customers in all enumerated places of public accommodation. And that construction would put an end to all obstructionist strategies and finally close one door on a bitter chapter in American history. . . .

DANIEL v. PAUL

395 U.S. 298 (1969)

Justice BRENNAN delivered the opinion of the Court [joined by Chief Justice WARREN, Justices DOUGLAS, HARLAN, STEWART, WHITE, FORTAS, and MARSHALL]:

. . . .

Lake Nixon Club, located 12 miles west of Little Rock, is a 232-acre amusement area with swimming, boating, sun bathing, picnicking, miniature golf, dancing facilities, and a snack bar. The Pauls purchased the Lake Nixon site in 1962 and subsequently operated this amusement business there in a racially segregated manner.

Title II of the Civil Rights Act . . . does not extend to private clubs. But, as both courts below properly found, Lake Nixon is not a private club. It is simply a business operated for a profit with none of the attributes of self-government and member-ownership traditionally associated with private clubs. It is true that following enactment of the Civil Rights Act of 1964, the Pauls began to refer to the establishment as a private club. They even began to require patrons to pay a 25-cent "membership" fee which gains a purchaser a "membership" card entitling him to enter the Club's premises for an entire season and, on payment of specified additional fees, to use the swimming, boating and miniature golf facilities. But this "membership" device seems no more than a subterfuge designed to avoid coverage of the 1964 [Civil Rights] Act. White persons are routinely provided "membership" cards, and some 100,000 whites visit the establishment each season. As the District Court found, Lake Nixon is "open in general to all of the public who are members of the white race." . . . Negroes, on the other hand, are uniformly denied "membership" cards, and thus admission, because of the Pauls' fear that integration would "ruin" the "business." The conclusion of the courts below that Lake Nixon is not a private club is plainly correct—indeed, respondent does not challenge that conclusion here.

We therefore turn to the question whether [the] Lake Nixon Club['s] . . . operation[s] "affect commerce" within the mean of [the Act]. . . .

The Pauls advertise the Lake Nixon Club in a monthly magazine called "Little Rock Today," which is distributed to guests at Little Rock hotels, motels, and restaurants, to acquaint them with available tourist attractions in the area. . . . Thus, the Lake Nixon Club unquestionably offered to serve out-of-state visitors to the Little Rock area. And it would be unrealistic to assume that none of the 100,000 patrons actually served by the Club each season was an interstate traveler. . . .

The record, although not as complete on this point as might be desired, also demonstrates that a "substantial portion of the food" served by the Lake Nixon Club snack bar has moved in interstate commerce. The snack bar serves a limited fare—hot dogs and hamburgers on buns, soft drinks, and milk. The District Court took judicial notice of the fact that the "principal ingredients going into the bread were produced and processed in other States" and that "certain ingredients [of the soft drinks] were probably obtained . . . from out-of-State sources." . . . Thus, at the very least, three of the four food items sold at the snack bar contain ingredients originating outside the State. There can be no serious doubt that a "substantial portion of the food" served at the snack bar has moved in interstate commerce. . . .

The remaining question is whether the operations of the Lake Nixon Club "affect commerce" within the meaning of [section] 201(c)(3). We conclude that they do. Lake Nixon's customary "sources of entertainment . . . move in commerce." The Club leases 15 paddle boats on a royalty basis from an Oklahoma company. Another boat was purchased from the same company. The Club's juke box was manufactured outside Arkansas and plays records manufactured outside the State. The legislative history indicates that mechanical sources of entertainment such as these were considered by Congress to be "sources of entertainment" within the meaning of [section] 201(c)(3). . . .

Justice BLACK dissenting:

. . . In order, therefore, for the Act to be held to apply the test must be shown to be met by evidence and judicial findings, not by guesswork, or assumptions, or "judicial knowledge" of crucially relevant facts, or by unproved probabilities or possibilities. My trouble with the Court's holding is that it runs roughshod over District Court findings supported by the record and emphatically affirmed by the Court of Appeals. . . .

(A) Did Lake Nixon serve or offer to serve interstate travelers? There is not a word of evidence showing that such an interstate traveler was ever there or ever invited there or ever dreamed of going there. Lake Nixon can be reached only by country roads. The record fails to show whether these country roads are passable in all kinds of weather. They seem to be at least six or eight miles off the state or interstate roads over which interstate travelers are accustomed to travel. . . .

. . . [T]his court jumps from the fact that there were an estimated number of admissions onto the club premises during a season to the conclusion that some one or more of these was an "interstate traveler" and that the owners of the premises, Mr. and Mrs. Paul, were bound to know that there were interstate travelers. That conclusion is far too speculative to be used as a means of rejecting the solemn findings of the two courts below. If the facts here are to be left to such "iffy" conjectures, one familiar with country life and traveling would, it seems to me, far more likely conclude that travelers on interstate journeys would stick to their interstate highways, and not go miles off them by way of what, for all this record shows, may well be dusty, unpaved, "country" roads to go to a purely local swimming hole where the only food they could buy was hamburgers, hot dogs, milk, and soft drinks (but not beer). This is certainly not the pattern of interstate movements I would expect interstate travelers in search of tourist attractions to follow.

(B) The second prong of the test to determine applicability of the Act to Lake Nixon is whether a "substantial portion" of the hamburgers, milk, and soda pop sold there had previously moved in interstate commerce. The Court's opinion generously concedes that the record is "not as complete on this point as might be desired. . . ." This is certainly no exaggeration. In fact, I would go further and agree with the two courts below that the record is totally devoid of evidence to show that a "substantial portion" of the small amount of food sold had previously moved in interstate commerce. . . . Fact-findings on serious problems like this one, which involves marking the jurisdictional authority of State and Nation, should not be made on the basis of "judicial notice" and on probabilities not based on evidence. . . .

Finally, the Court mentions, almost as an afterthought, Lake Nixon's 15 paddle boats leased from an Oklahoma company on a royalty basis. As to these paddle boats the Court of Appeals said: "It is common knowledge that annually thousands of this type boat are manufactured locally in Arkansas, and there is no evidence whatsoever that any of the equipment moved in interstate commerce." . . .

It seems clear to me that neither the paddle boats nor the locally leased juke box is sufficient to justify holding that the operation of Lake Nixon affects interstate commerce within the meaning of the Act. While it is the duty of courts to enforce this important Act, we are not called on to hold nor should we hold subject to that Act this country people's recreation center, lying in what may be, so far as we know, a little "sleepy hollow" between Arkansas hills miles away from any interstate highway. This would be stretching the Commerce Clause so as to give the Federal Government complete control over every little nook and cranny of every precinct and county in every one of the 50 States. This goes too far for me. . . .

Questions

1. Attorney General Kennedy asserted that businesses would know if they are covered by the Act. Was he correct? Why did Kennedy stumble when attempting to respond to Sen. Thurmond's questions about the circumstances in which a business would be covered? If Kennedy's assertion was not correct, did he misperceive the clarity of the statute or was he merely providing Congress with tactical reassurance to assist the passage of the Act?
2. Was Attorney General Kennedy correct in claiming that the statute did not effectively extend congressional power under the Commerce Clause?
3. In retrospect, how would you assess Sen. Thurmond's analogy between antidiscrimination laws and Prohibition? Has the public accepted Title II?
4. The Supreme Court has the authority to reverse its own long-standing precedents. For example, *Brown v. Board of Education* in 1954 reversed the "separate but equal" precedent in *Plessy v. Ferguson* (1896) that had endorsed official segregation. Why did the Supreme Court choose *not* to uphold the statute under the Fourteenth Amendment by reversing the *Civil Rights Cases*? Was Justice Douglas correct in claiming that utilization of the Fourteenth Amendment would solve any problems concerning the application of the statute?

5. Archibald Cox writes that "[t]he decision sustaining the application of the federal statute to Ollie's choice of customers as a regulation of interstate commerce strikes many nonlawyers as a complete distortion of the words 'to regulate commerce . . . among the several states' [in Article I, section 8 of the Constitution], just as it shocks law students until their professors corrupt them."[3] What does Cox mean by saying people are "shock[ed]" by the decision? What does he mean when he says law students become "corrupt[ed]"?

6. In *Katzenbach/Heart of Atlanta*, Justice Black noted that congressional power under the Commerce Clause applies to individuals' economic activities within states because of the aggregate effect such activities may have on interstate commerce. If Congress can apply this civil rights law to small commercial actors within states, are there any commerce-related activities that Congress *cannot* regulate under the Commerce Clause?

7. Why did Justice Black dissent in *Daniel v. Paul*? Was his dissent inconsistent with the theory of Commerce Clause power that he espoused in *Katzenbach/Heart of Atlanta*?

8. In *Daniel*, was the Supreme Court more concerned with the facts regarding the Club's connection to interstate commerce or the plain fact that the Club engaged in racial discrimination?

9. Why did the Supreme Court merely *assume* that the Club was connected to interstate commerce without requiring evidence proving the purported connections? Is this a proper approach for a court to take in finding relevant facts?

10. What message would society receive if the authors of *Brown v. Board of Education* (i.e., the Supreme Court) endorsed Black's dissent in *Daniel*? What would have been the political consequences of such a decision?

11. Were there any possible circumstances in which the Supreme Court would have recognized a business as *outside* of the Act and therefore able to engage in racial discrimination legally? Is your answer affected by assessing the Court's composition? (How many holdovers were there from *Brown v. Board of Education*? Who were the other justices and which presidents appointed them?)

12. The Supreme Court's symbolic statement in *Brown* in 1954 helped to mobilize and encourage various actors in the political system to push for racial equality. The Civil Rights Act of 1964 represented the moment when the other branches of government finally acted to endorse unambiguously the racial equality goals espoused by the Supreme Court one decade earlier. At that historical moment, could the Supreme Court have decided these cases any other way? Given the convergence of historical forces and political institutions, was this the best opportunity to broaden the scope of the Fourteenth Amendment to cover private actors? What would have been the political consequences of a Court decision to uphold the Act under the Fourteenth Amendment?

3. Archibald Cox, *The Warren Court: Constitutional Decision as an Instrument of Reform* (Cambridge, MA: Harvard University Press, 1968), p. 52.

FIVE

The Evolution of Constitutional Interpretation

The United States Constitution is a relatively brief document upon which to base the structure and distribution of government power within a complex, twentieth-century society. Because the twenty-six amendments to the Constitution address only specific, narrow topics, most of the language in the Constitution—language that continues to govern the country—remains intact from when it was written in 1787. One of the great, continuing debates in constitutional law is over the appropriate method for interpreting and applying these words in order to govern contemporary American society properly.

During the 1980s, this debate became more open and vigorous than ever through public exchanges between Attorney General Edwin Meese and Justice William Brennan, and through the controversial Senate hearings on the unsuccessful nomination of Judge Robert Bork to the Supreme Court. Meese and Bork asserted that the Constitution should be interpreted through "original intent" by following the specific intentions of the eighteenth-century men who wrote the document. By contrast, Justice Brennan conceived of the Constitution as a flexible document embodying ideals of human dignity that will grow and change as society evolves through history.

The "original intent" theory is attractive because it potentially provides a basis for limiting judicial power by ensuring that judges adhere to a commonly accepted, restrained approach to constitutional interpretation. Despite its attractiveness in theory, there are serious problems involved in identifying the "original intent" of the authors in many provisions of this brief, two hundred year-old document containing ambiguity and compromises.[1]

---

1. *See* Stephen Macedo, *The New Right v. The Constitution* (Washington, D.C.: The Cato Institute, 1987); Judith A. Baer, "The Fruitless Search for Original Intent," in *Judging the Constitution: Critical Essays on Judicial Lawmaking,* eds. Michael W. McCann and Gerald L. Houseman (Glenview, IL: Scott, Foresman and Co., 1989), pp. 49-71.

Although many advocates of "original intent" have themselves deviated from the theory,[2] they have struggled to avoid acknowledging the theory's weaknesses. Whatever the merits or flaws of this normative theory, it is clear that, descriptively, the human beings who have served as Supreme Court justices have actually interpreted the Constitution in a flexible manner. The meaning of the Constitution changes as justices interpret its words in conjunction with historical, social, and political developments in American society.

Although it disappoints idealists to recognize that the justices do not now and have never interpreted the Constitution according to any neutral, pure theory of law, such a realization should not breed cynicism about constitutional law. Constitutional law is not merely the product of justices' narrowly self-interested or idiosyncratic whims, but instead is intimately related to the political and social evolution of American society.

The cases and questions reprinted in this chapter illustrate the evolutionary nature of constitutional interpretation by focusing on the process through which the provisions of the Bill of Rights were applied to the states. In the 1833 case of *Barron v. Baltimore*, the Supreme Court declared that the Bill of Rights did not protect individuals' rights against encroachment by the states. Mr. Barron's wharf was inadvertently wrecked as a consequence of road construction work undertaken by the City of Baltimore. He asserted that he had been deprived of property by the local government in contravention of the Fifth Amendment and therefore deserved "just compensation." Chief Justice John Marshall decreed, however, that the Fifth Amendment and other provisions of the Bill of Rights applied only against actions by the federal government.

The passage of the Fourteenth Amendment created protections for individuals' rights against actions by the states. These protections, however, were not phrased in the specific language of the Bill of Rights (e.g., freedom of speech, right to counsel, etc.), but instead were couched in terms of vague, general rights: "privileges or immunities of citizens," "due process of law," and "equal protection of the law." Although scholars subsequently argued that the Fourteenth Amendment was intended to apply the specific provisions of the Bill of Rights to the states, the Supreme Court initially rejected that view.[3]

As shown in the cases that follow, the Supreme Court struggled with the process of giving meaning to the rights contained in the Fourteenth Amendment. In 1897, the Court declared that the Fourteenth Amend-

2. Christopher E. Smith, "Jurisprudential Politics and the Manipulation of History," *The Western Journal of Black Studies* (1989) 13: 156–161.

3. Henry J. Abraham, *Freedom and the Court: Civil Rights and Liberties in the United States*, 5th ed. (New York: Oxford University Press, 1988), pp. 38–117.

ment provided due process rights to protect people's property in a fashion similar to the Fifth Amendment's due process property rights (*Chicago, Burlington and Quincy Railroad v. Chicago*). The Fifth and Fourteenth Amendments protect against deprivations of life, liberty, or property without due process of law by federal and state governments respectively. This initial recognition of individuals' rights against the states was based upon the straightforward, parallel language contained in the Bill of Rights and in the Fourteenth Amendment.

Subsequently, in 1925, the Supreme Court expanded the scope of individual rights by noting that free speech was a fundamental liberty contained in the concept of "due process" in the Fourteenth Amendment which states could not infringe (*Gitlow v. New York*). This recognition of individuals' rights was based not upon explicit words in the Constitution, but upon the justices' interpretation of basic rights protected by the document's general provisions. Having decided that free speech was protected from state action, despite the absence of specific words to that effect in the Fourteenth Amendment, the Supreme Court was confronted with the problem of determining which other rights from the Bill of Rights were also applicable to the states through the Due Process Clause of the Fourteenth Amendment. In the mid-twentieth century, the gradual incorporation of rights from the Bill of Rights for application to the states reflected historical developments as the justices of the Supreme Court and the American citizenry placed greater emphasis upon protecting individuals from intrusive, repressive, and discriminatory actions by state and local governments.

PALKO v. CONNECTICUT

302 U.S. 319 (1937)

Justice CARDOZO delivered the opinion of the Court [joined by Chief Justice HUGHES, Justices BLACK, McREYNOLDS, BRANDEIS, SUTHERLAND, ROBERTS, and STONE. Justice BUTLER dissented.]:

A statute of Connecticut permitting appeals in criminal cases to be taken by the state is challenged by appellant as an infringement of the Fourteenth Amendment. . . .

Appellant was indicted in Fairfield County, Conn., for the crime of murder in the first degree. A jury found him guilty of murder in the second degree, and he was sentenced to confinement in the state prison for life. Thereafter the State of Connecticut, with the permission of the judge presiding at trial gave notice of appeal to the Supreme Court [of

Connecticut] . . . [which] reversed the judgment and ordered a new trial [due to improperly excluded testimony and improper jury instructions]. . . . [Palko] made the objection that the effect of the new trial was to place him twice in jeopardy for the same offense, and in so doing, violate the Fourteenth Amendment. . . . [T]he [second] trial proceeded [and] [t]he jury returned a verdict of murder in the first degree, and the Court sentenced the defendant to the punishment of death. . . .

The argument for appellant is that whatever is forbidden by the Fifth Amendment is forbidden by the Fourteenth also. The Fifth Amendment, which is not directed to the States, but solely to the federal government, creates immunity from double jeopardy. . . . The Fourteenth Amendment ordains, "nor shall any state deprive any person of life, liberty, or property, without due process of law." To retry a defendant, though under one indictment and only one, subjects him, it is said, to double jeopardy in violation of the Fifth Amendment, if the prosecution is one on behalf of the United States. From this the consequence is said to follow that there is a denial of life or liberty without due process of law, if the prosecution is one on behalf of the people of a state. . . .

. . . [Palko's] thesis is even broader. Whatever would be a violation of the original bill of rights (Amendments 1 to 8) if done by the federal government is now equally unlawful by force of the Fourteenth Amendment if done by a state. There is no such general rule. . . .

The line of division may seem to be wavering and broken if there is a hasty catalogue of the cases on the one side [supporting] and the other [opposing the application of specific rights to the states]. Reflection and analysis will induce a different view. There emerges a perception of a rationalizing principle which gives to discrete instances a proper order and coherence. The right to trial by jury and the immunity from prosecution except as the result of an indictment have value and importance. Even so, they are not of the very essence of a scheme of ordered liberty. To abolish them is not to violate a "principle of justice so rooted in the traditions and conscience of our people as to be ranked as fundamental." . . . Few would be so narrow or provincial as to maintain that a fair and enlightened system of justice would be impossible without them. What is true of jury trials and indictments is true also, as the cases show, of the immunity from compulsory self-incrimination. . . . This too might be lost, and justice still be done. . . . The exclusion of these immunities and privileges from the privileges and immunities protected against the action of the States has not been arbitrary or casual. It has been dictated by a study and appreciation of the meaning, the essential implications, of liberty itself.

We reach a different plane of social and moral values when we pass to the privileges and immunities that have been taken over from the earlier articles of the Federal Bill of Rights and brought within the Fourteenth Amendment by the process of absorption. These in their origin were effective against the federal government alone. If the Fourteenth Amendment has absorbed them, the process of absorption has had its source in the belief that neither liberty nor justice would exist if they were sacrificed. . . . This is true, for illustration, of freedom of thought and speech. Of that freedom one may say that it is the matrix, the indispensable condition, of nearly every other form of freedom. . . .

. . . Is that kind of double jeopardy to which the statute has subjected [Palko] a hardship so acute and shocking that our polity will not endure it? Does it violate those "fundamental principles of liberty and justice which lie at the base of all our civil and political institutions"? . . . The answer surely must be "no." What the answer would have to be if the state were permitted after a trial free from error to try the accused over again or to bring another case against him, we have no occasion to consider. We deal with the statute before us and no other. The state is not attempting to wear the accused out by a multitude of cases with accumulated trials. It asks no more than this, that the case against him shall go on until there shall be a trial free from the corrosion of substantial legal error. . . .

ADAMSON v. CALIFORNIA

332 U.S. 46 (1947)

Justice REED delivered the opinion of the Court [joined by Chief Justice VINSON, Justices FRANKFURTER, BURTON, and JACKSON]:

The appellant, Adamson, a citizen of the United States, was convicted, without recommendation for mercy, by jury in a Superior Court of the State of California. . . . The provisions of California law which were challenged in state proceedings as invalid under the Fourteenth Amendment to the Federal Constitution are those of the state constitution and penal code . . . [which] permit the failure of a defendant to explain or to deny evidence against him to be commented upon by court and by counsel and to be considered by court and jury. The defendant did not testify. . . .

. . . [I]f the defendant, after answering affirmatively charges alleging prior convictions, takes the witness stand to deny or explain other evidence that has been introduced "the commission of these crimes could have been revealed to the jury on cross-examination to impeach his testimony." . . . This forces an accused who is a repeat offender to choose between the risk of having his prior offenses disclosed to the jury or of having it draw harmful inferences from uncontradicted evidence that can only be denied or explained by the defendant. . . .

We shall assume, but without any intention thereby of ruling upon the issue, that state permission by law to the court, counsel and jury to comment upon and consider the failure of defendant "to explain or to deny by his testimony any evidence or facts in the case against him" would infringe defendant's privilege against self-incrimination under the Fifth Amendment if this were a trial in a [federal] court. . . . Such an assumption does not determine appellant's rights under the Fourteenth Amendment [because] [i]t is settled law that the [self-incrimination protection] of the Fifth Amendment . . . is not made effective by the Fourteenth Amendment as a protection against state action. . . .

. . . A right to a fair trial is a right admittedly protected by the due process clause of the Fourteenth Amendment. Therefore, appellant argues, the due process clause of the Fourteenth Amendment protects his privilege against self-incrimination. The due process clause of the Fourteenth Amendment, however, does not draw all the rights of the federal Bill of Rights under its protection. That contention was made and rejected in *Palko v. Connecticut*. . . . Nothing has been called to our attention that either the framers of the Fourteenth Amendment or the states that adopted it intended its due process clause to draw within its scope the earlier amendments to the Constitution. *Palko* held that such provisions of the Bill of Rights as were "implicit in the concept of ordered liberty" . . . became secure from state interference by the clause. But it held nothing more.

Specifically the due process clause does not protect by virtue of its mere existence, the accused's freedom from giving testimony by compulsion in state trials that is secured to him against federal interference by the Fifth Amendment. . . . For a state to require testimony from an accused is not necessarily a breach of a state's obligation to give a fair trial.

. . .

It is true that if comment were forbidden an accused in this situation could remain silent and avoid evidence of former crimes and comment upon his failure to testify. We are of the view, however, that a state may control such a situation in accordance with its own ideas of the most efficient administration of criminal justice. The purpose of due process is not to protect an accused against a proper conviction but against an unfair conviction. When evidence is before a jury that threatens conviction, it does not seem unfair to require him to choose between leaving the adverse evidence unexplained and subjecting himself to impeachment through disclosure of former crimes. . . .

Justice BLACK dissenting [joined by Justice DOUGLAS]:

. . . .

This decision reasserts a constitutional theory . . . that this Court is endowed by the Constitution with boundless power under "natural law" periodically to expand and contract constitutional standards to conform to the Court's conception of what at a particular time constitutes "civilized decency" and "fundamental liberty and justice." Invoking this . . . rule, the Court concludes that although comment upon testimony in a federal court would violate the Fifth Amendment, identical comment in a state court does not violate today's fashion in civilized decency and fundamentals and is therefore not prohibited by the Federal Constitution as amended. . . . I think the decision and the "natural law" theory of the Constitution upon which it relies degrade the constitutional safeguards of the Bill of Rights and simultaneously appropriate for this Court a broad power which we are not authorized by the Constitution to exercise. . . .

My study of the historical events that culminated in the Fourteenth Amendment, and the expressions of those who sponsored and favored, as well as those who opposed its submission and passage, persuades me that one of the chief objects that the provisions of the Amendment's first section, separately, and as a whole, were intended to accomplish was to make the Bill of Rights applicable to the states. With full knowledge of the import of the *Barron* decision, the framers and backers of the Fourteenth Amendment proclaimed its purpose to be to overturn the constitutional rule that case had announced. This historical purpose has never received full consideration or exposition in any opinion of the Court interpreting the Amendment. . . .

. . . [T]he [Bill of Rights' provisions are designed to protect against] the same kind of human evils that have emerged from century to century wherever excessive power is sought by the few at the expense of the many. In my judgment the people of no nation can lose their liberty so long as a Bill of Rights like ours survives and its basic purposes are conscientiously interpreted, enforced, and respected so as to afford continuous protections against old, as well as new, devices and practices which might thwart those purposes. I fear to see the consequences of the Court's practice of substituting its own concepts of decency and fundamental justice for the language of the Bill of Rights as its point of departure in interpreting and enforcing that Bill of Rights. If the choice is between the selective process of the *Palko* decision applying some of the Bill of Rights to the States, or the rule . . . applying none, I would choose the *Palko* process. But rather than accept either of these choices, I would follow what I believe was the original purpose of the Fourteenth Amendment—to extend to all the people of the nation the complete protections of the Bill of Rights.

Justice MURPHY dissenting [joined by Justice RUTLEDGE]:

While in substantial agreement with the views of Mr. Justice Black, I have one reservation and one addition. I agree that the specific guarantees of the Bill of Rights should be carried over intact into the first section of the Fourteenth Amendment. But I am not prepared to say that the latter is entirely and necessarily limited by the Bill of Rights. Occasions may arise where a proceeding falls so far short of conforming to fundamental standards of procedure as to warrant constitutional condemnation in terms of a lack of due process despite the absence of a specific provision in the Bill of Rights.

ROCHIN v. CALIFORNIA

342 U.S. 165 (1952)

Justice FRANKFURTER delivered the opinion of the Court [joined by Chief Justice VINSON, Justices CLARK, REED, BURTON, and JACKSON. Justice MINTON did not participate.]:

Having "some information that [Rochin] was selling narcotics," three deputy sheriffs of the County of Los Angeles, on the morning of July 1, 1949, made for the two-story dwelling house in which Rochin lived with his mother, common-law wife, brothers and sisters. Finding the outside door open, they entered and then forced open the door to Rochin's room on the second floor. Inside they found petitioner, sitting partly dressed on the side of the bed, upon which his wife was lying. On a "night stand" beside the bed the deputies spied two capsules. When asked "Whose stuff is this?" Rochin seized the capsules and put them in his mouth. A struggle ensued, in the course of which the three officers "jumped upon him" and attempted to extract the capsules. The force they applied proved unavailing against Rochin's resistance. He was handcuffed and taken to a hospital. At the direction of one of the officers a doctor forced an emetic solution through a tube into Rochin's stomach against his will. This "stomach pumping" produced vomiting. In the vomited matter were found two capsules which proved to contain morphine. [Rochin was convicted of possessing morphine based upon the two capsules]. . . .

On appeal, the District Court of Appeals affirmed the conviction, despite the finding that the officers "were guilty of unlawfully breaking into and entering defendant's room and were guilty of unlawfully assaulting and battering defendant while in the room," and "were guilty of unlawfully assaulting, battering, torturing and falsely imprisoning the defendant at the alleged hospital." . . .

[Although obligated to defer to the states on matters of criminal justice administration,] this Court too has its responsibility. Regard for the requirements of the Due Process Clause [of the Fourteenth Amendment] "inescapably imposes upon this Court an exercise of judgment . . . in order to ascertain whether [state procedures] offend those canons of decency and fairness which express the notions of justice of English-speaking peoples even toward those charged with the most heinous offenses." . . . These standards of justice are not authoritatively formulated anywhere as though they were specifics. Due process of law is a summarized constitutional guarantee of respect for those personal immunities which, as Mr. Justice Cardozo twice wrote for the Court, are "so rooted in the traditions and conscience of our people as to be ranked as fundamental," . . . or are "implicit in the concept of ordered liberty." *Palko v. State of Connecticut.* . . .

Applying these general considerations to the circumstances of the present case, we are compelled to conclude that the proceedings by which this conviction was obtained do more than offend some fastidious squeamishness or private sentimentalism about combatting crime too energetically. This is conduct that shocks the conscience. Illegally breaking into the privacy of the petitioner, the struggle to open his mouth and remove what was there, the forcible extraction of his stomach's contents—this course of proceedings by agents of government to obtain evidence is bound to offend even hardened sensibilities. They are methods too close to the rack and the screw to permit of constitutional differentiation. . . .

. . . So here, to sanction the brutal conduct which naturally was condemned by the court whose judgment is before us, would be to afford brutality the cloak of law. Nothing would be more calculated to discredit law and thereby to brutalize the temper of society. . . .

Justice BLACK concurring:

Adamson v. California . . . sets forth reasons for my belief that state as well as federal courts and law enforcement officers must obey the Fifth Amendment's command [against self-incrimination]. . . . I think a person is compelled to be a witness against himself . . . when as here, incriminating evidence is forcibly taken from him by a contrivance of modern science.

Justice DOUGLAS concurring:

. . . .

As an original matter it might be debatable whether the provision in the Fifth Amendment that no person "shall be compelled in any criminal case to be a witness against himself" serves the ends of justice. Not all civilized legal procedures [in Europe] recognize it. But the choice was made by the Framers, a choice which sets a standard for legal trials in this country. The Framers made it a standard of due process for a trial in a federal courthouse. If it is a requirement of due process for a trial in the federal courthouse, it is impossible for me to say it is not a requirement of due process for a trial in the state courthouse. . . .

DUNCAN v. LOUISIANA

391 U.S. 145 (1968)

Justice WHITE delivered the opinion of the Court [joined by Chief Justice WARREN, Justices BLACK, DOUGLAS, BRENNAN, MARSHALL, and FORTAS]:

Appellant, Gary Duncan was convicted of simple battery[,] . . . a misdemeanor, punishable by a maximum of two years' imprisonment and a $300 fine. Appellant sought trial by jury, but because the Louisiana Constitution grants jury trials only in cases in which capital punishment or imprisonment at hard labor may be imposed, the trial judge denied the request. Appellant was convicted and sentenced to serve 60 days in the parish prison and pay a fine of $150. . . . [A]ppellant sought review in this Court, alleging that the Sixth and Fourteenth Amendments to the United States Constitution secure the right to jury trial in state criminal prosecutions. . . .

Appellant was 19 years of age when tried. While driving down Highway 23 in Plaquemines Parish on October 18, 1966, he saw two younger cousins engaged in a conversation by the side of the road with four white boys. Knowing his cousins, Negroes who had recently transferred to a formerly all-white high school, had reported the occurrence of racial incidents at the school, Duncan stopped the car, got out, and approached the six boys. At the trial the white boys and a white onlooker testified, as did appellant and his cousins. The testimony was in dispute on many points, but the witnesses agreed that appellant and the white boys spoke to each other, that appellant encouraged his cousins to break off the encounter and enter his car, and appellant was about to enter the car himself for the purpose of driving away with his cousins. The whites testified that just before getting in the car appellant slapped Herman Landry, one of the white boys, on the elbow. The Negroes testified that appellant had not slapped Landry, but had merely touched him. The trial judge concluded that the State had proved beyond a reasonable doubt that Duncan had committed simple battery, and found him guilty.

I

The Fourteenth Amendment denies the States the power to "deprive any person of life, liberty, or property, without due process of law." In resolving conflicting claims concerning the meaning of this spacious language, the Court has looked increasingly to the Bill of Rights for guidance; many of the rights guaranteed by the first eight Amendments to the Constitution have been held to be protected against state action by the Due Process Clause of the Fourteenth Amendment. That clause now protects the right to compensation for property taken by the State; the rights to speech, press, and religion covered by the First Amendment; the Fourteenth Amendment rights to be free from unreasonable searches and seizures and to have excluded from criminal trials any evidence illegally seized; the right guaranteed by the Fifth Amendment to be free of compelled self-incrimination; and the Sixth Amendment rights to counsel, to a speedy and public trial, to confrontation of opposing witnesses, and to compulsory process for obtaining witnesses. . . .

. . . Because we believe that trial by jury in criminal cases is fundamental to the American scheme of justice, we hold that the Fourteenth Amendment guarantees a right of jury trial in all criminal cases which—were they to be tried in federal court—would come within the Sixth Amendment's guarantee.[14]

14. In one sense, recent cases applying provisions of the first eight Amendments to the States represent a new approach to the "incorporation" debate. Earlier the Court can be seen as having asked, when inquiring whether some particular procedural safeguard was required of a State, if a civilized system could be imagined that would not accord the particular protection. For example, *Palko v. State of Connecticut* . . . stated: "The right to trial by jury . . . may have value and importance. Even so, they are not of the very essence of a scheme of ordered liberty. . . . Few would be so narrow or provincial as to maintain that a fair and enlightened system of justice would be impossible without them." The recent cases, on the other hand, have proceeded upon the valid assumption that state criminal processes are not imaginary and theoretical schemes but actual systems bearing virtually every characteristic of the common-law system that has been developing contemporaneously in England and in this country. The question thus is whether given this kind of system a particular procedure is fundamental—whether, that is, a procedure is necessary to an Anglo-American regime of ordered liberty. . . . [T]he question is not necessarily fundamental to fairness in every criminal system that might be imagined but is fundamental in the context of the criminal processes maintained by the American States.

. . . A criminal process which was fair and equitable but used no juries is easy to imagine. It would make use of alternative guarantees and protections. . . . Yet no American system has undertaken to construct such a system. . . .

We are aware of prior cases in this Court in which the prevailing opinion contains statements to the contrary to our holding today that the
right to jury trial in serious criminal cases is a fundamental right and
hence must be recognized by the States as part of their obligation to extend due process of law to all persons within their jurisdiction. . . . [How-
ever,] [i]n neither *Palko* nor *Snyder* [*v. Massachusetts* (1934)] was jury trial
actually at issue, although both cases contain important dicta asserting
that the right to jury trial is not essential to ordered liberty. . . . These
observations, though weighty and respectable, are nevertheless dicta, un-
supported by holdings in this Court that a State may refuse a defendant's
demand for a jury trial when he is charged with a serious crime. . . . Respectfully, we reject the prior dicta regarding jury trial in criminal cases.
. . .

Justice BLACK concurring [joined by Justice DOUGLAS]:

. . . With [today's] holding I agree for reasons given by the Court. I also
agree because of reasons given in my dissent in *Adamson v. California*. . . .
In that dissent, . . . I took the position . . . that the Fourteenth Amendment made all of the provisions of the Bill of Rights applicable to the
States. . . . And I am very happy to support this selective process through
which our Court has since the *Adamson* case held most of the specific Bill
of Rights' protections applicable to the States to the same extent they are
applicable to the Federal Government. . . .

Justice HARLAN dissenting [joined by Justice STEWART]:

. . . The Due Process Clause of the Fourteenth Amendment requires that
those procedures be fundamentally fair in all respects. It does not, in my
view, impose or encourage nationwide uniformity for its own sake; it does
not command adherence to forms that happen to be old; and it does not
impose on the States the rules that may be in force in the federal courts
except where such rules are also found to be essential to basic fairness.
     The Court's approach to this case is an uneasy and illogical compro-
mise among the views of the various Justices on how the Due Process
Clause should be interpreted. . . .
     I have raised my voice many times before against the Court's contin-
uing undiscriminating insistence upon fastening on the States federal notions of criminal justice, and I must do so again in this instance. With all
respect, the Court's approach and its reading of history are altogether
topsy-turvy.

I

I believe I am correct in saying that every member of the Court for at least the last 135 years has agreed that our Founders did not consider the requirements of the Bill of Rights so fundamental that they should operate directly against the states. . . .

A few members of the Court have taken the position that the intention of those who drafted the first section of the Fourteenth Amendment was simply, and exclusively, to make the provisions of the first eight Amendments applicable to state action. This view has never been accepted by this Court. . . .

Today's Court still remains unwilling to accept the total incorporationists' view of the history of the Fourteenth Amendment. This, if accepted, would afford a cogent reason for applying the Sixth Amendment to the States. The Court is also, apparently, unwilling to face the task of determining whether denial of trial by jury in the situation before us, or in other situations, is fundamentally unfair. Consequently, the Court has compromised on the ease of the incorporationist position, without its internal logic. It has simply assumed that the question before us is whether the Jury Trial Clause of the Sixth Amendment should be incorporated into the Fourteenth, jot-for-jot, and case-for-case, or ignored. Then the Court merely declares that the Clause is "in" rather than "out." . . .

Questions

1. Why is Cardozo's opinion in *Palko* considered by many people to be a major "advance" in the protection of individuals' constitutional rights? [NOTE: It is ironic that many important cases advancing the development of individual rights actually resulted in severe punishments for the individuals involved in the cases. Palko was executed after his second trial and unsuccessful appeal. Similarly, Gitlow received a prison sentence although his case (*Gitlow v. New York*, 1925) served as the initial vehicle for the Supreme Court to apply free speech rights to the states].
2. Justice Frankfurter (in *Rochin*) and Justice Harlan (in *Duncan*) claim to follow Cardozo's *Palko* precedent in assessing which rights apply against the states. Is their approach the same as Cardozo's? Is it significant that Cardozo writes of "privileges and immunities that have been brought over from . . . the Federal Bill of Rights . . . by the process of absorption"? How does Justice Harlan regard the process of incorporation (i.e., "absorption")?
3. What is Justice Black's approach for determining which rights apply to the states? Is Black consistent in the application of his theory in *Adamson, Rochin,* and *Duncan*?
4. What is Justice Murphy's theory? How is it different from Justice Black's?
5. What is Justice Frankfurter's approach in *Rochin*? How can a judge tell if something "shocks the conscience"? Can such determinations be based

upon principle or merely upon justices' individual reactions? Would it "shock the conscience" for the police to break illegally into the home of someone who assassinated the president of the United States? Would it "shock the conscience" for the police to break illegally into the home of someone with unpaid traffic tickets? Will justices' reactions or "conscience[s]" differ at different moments in history?

6. What is Justice White's approach to applying rights against the states? Is it the same approach as that applied by Cardozo in *Palko*?

7. Of all the approaches advocated by justices in these cases, which one "prevailed" in actually determining how rights would be applied to the states?

8. If *Palko* established the significant precedent for subsequent cases and *Palko* specifically stated that a right to trial by jury is *not* fundamental, how can Justice White reach the opposite conclusion in *Duncan* without reversing *Palko*?

9. Except for the nineteenth-century case on property rights (*Chicago, Burlington and Quincy Railroad v. Chicago*, 1897), the first time that the Supreme Court applied provisions of the Bill of Rights to the States through the Fourteenth Amendment was in 1925 (*Gitlow v. New York*). In effect, contrary to many Americans' cherished notions about the Bill of Rights guaranteeing individuals' freedom since 1791, most constitutional rights were actually unprotected against infringements by state and local governments until the middle of the twentieth century. How many rights had been applied against the states by 1968?

10. If the Fourteenth Amendment's words meant something specific to the authors of those words in the 1860s (and presumably they did), is it right for the Supreme Court justices in later decades to change the meaning of those words?

11. The facts and relatively harsh punishment in *Duncan* illustrate the manner in which the judicial system was utilized in many states to control and oppress African-Americans for most of American history. Was the justices' criminal justice decision in *Duncan* influenced by simultaneous developments in the Supreme Court's role as an institutional leader in society's movement toward racial equality?

SIX

The Politics of Capital Punishment

An important influence upon Supreme Court decisions and the development of constitutional law is the individual justices' policy preferences. The justices may have broad concerns about the societal policy implications of particular legal rules or, more narrowly, they may desire to achieve a particular outcome in a specific case. For example, Justice Rehnquist, prior to his elevation to chief justice, wrote an opinion creating a "public safety" exception to the *Miranda* rules about informing criminal suspects of their rights (*New York v. Quarles*, 1984). Rehnquist applied a vague cost-benefit analysis to conclude that the policy goal of protecting the public from crime outweighed the goals of immediately informing suspects of their rights and providing police officers with clear rules to guide the treatment of suspects during arrests. As in other decisions by the Supreme Court, the outcome of the *Quarles* case was not determined by adherence to a particular legal theory. Instead, the result was shaped by the justices' values and policy preferences. The justices' policy preferences are inevitable components of the human process of judicial decision making. As Harry Stumpf observes:

> [T]here exists no philosopher's stone of constitutional interpretation. Rather, it is a human process undertaken by human beings with human desires, motivations, feelings and failings. It is inevitable, then, that the Constitution will be read in the light of the philosophy of the reader, including his or her view of right and wrong, sound and unsound policy. It can be no other way.[1]

---

1. Harry P. Stumpf, *American Judicial Politics* (New York: Harcourt Brace Jovanovich, 1988), p.46.

The controversial issue of capital punishment provides illustrations of justices' strategic actions as they pursue their preferred policy objectives and their respective theories of constitutional interpretation.

There are legitimate philosophical disputes among the justices about how the Eighth Amendment's prohibition of "cruel and unusual punishments" affects the twentieth-century application of the death penalty. Justices Brennan and Marshall believed that capital punishment violates twentieth-century American values and therefore is forbidden by the Eighth Amendment. Their conclusion was based upon their view of the Constitution as a flexible document which embodies evolving ideals of human dignity. By contrast, Chief Justice Rehnquist and Justice Scalia believe that the Eighth Amendment does not prohibit the death penalty. They point to both the Framers' acceptance of capital punishment and the fact that most states have statutes endorsing the policy as evidence of the constitutionality of the death penalty. In attempting to identify the causal factors fueling this fundamental debate, it would be difficult to know whether the justices' viewpoints are attributable primarily to their judicial philosophies concerning the Eighth Amendment, or if their individual policy preferences are most influential.

Policy preferences can be identified, however, by focusing on the justices' actions rather than on the theories that they espouse. Chief Justice Rehnquist, for example, manifested his policy preference for expedited death penalty appeals and executions by clashing with other federal judges over recommendations to Congress concerning appellate procedures. Rehnquist appointed a committee headed by retired Justice Lewis Powell to propose reforms for the processing of appeals in capital cases. Rehnquist subsequently submitted the proposals for consideration by the Judicial Conference of the United States, the federal judges' policymaking body composed of judges representing the various judicial circuits. At its September 1989 meeting, the judges on the Judicial Conference decided to defer judgment on the proposals until their March 1990 meeting in order to discuss the proposals more fully with the other judges in their home circuits. After the September meeting, Rehnquist forwarded the proposals to Congress on behalf of the judiciary without waiting for discussion and endorsement by the other members of the Judicial Conference. In a rare public rebuke to the Chief Justice, fourteen judges, constituting a majority of the Judicial Conference, sent a letter to Congress disavowing the proposals and asserting that Rehnquist's views did not represent those of the other federal judges.[2] Subsequently, at its

---

2. Linda Greenhouse, "Judges Challenge Rehnquist Action on Death Penalty: An Extraordinary Move," *New York Times*, Oct. 6, 1989, pp. A1, B7.

March meeting, the Judicial Conference rejected Rehnquist's favored reforms and forwarded an alternative proposal to Congress which did not place such strict limits on the opportunities for death row inmates to contest their convictions.[3] Although judges usually keep their internal policy disputes secret, this conflict over capital punishment became a public illustration of judges' political interactions concerning their policy preferences.

Although the Judicial Conference and Congress did not support Rehnquist's desired reforms, the increasingly conservative majority on the Supreme Court acted through judicial decisions to expedite death penalty appeals. For example, in 1991 the Court sharply narrowed prisoners' ability to challenge errors in their trials (*McCleskey v. Zant*). Justice Marshall accused Rehnquist and the other members of the majority of "toss[ing] aside established precedents without explanations [and] disregard[ing] the will of Congress."

Capital punishment in the United States ceased in 1972 when the Supreme Court decided in *Furman v. Georgia* that the states' application of the death penalty unconstitutionally granted too much discretion to judges and juries. As a result, the punishment had been applied in an unfair, arbitrary manner. Many observers thought this was an initial step toward abolition of capital punishment, but the Supreme Court reactivated the death penalty in *Gregg v. Georgia* (1976) by requiring states to create clearer standards for application of the punishment. Subsequent Supreme Court cases have addressed various issues concerning the circumstances in which the death penalty can be applied.

The cases of *Enmund v. Florida* and *Tison v. Arizona*, which are reprinted in this chapter, illuminate the justices' interactions and policy preferences concerning the death penalty. In *Enmund*, a closely divided Court established a rule to determine when capital punishment can be applied to accomplices who do not directly commit a murder. In *Tison*, a closely divided Court expanded upon, and arguably changed, the rule created in *Enmund*. The strategic interactions within the Court are evident by comparing the two cases and the questions that follow.

Although the justices have philosophical disagreements about whether the Eighth Amendment prohibits the death penalty, all of the justices agree that capital punishment should be applied in accordance with the principles of "due process" and "equal protection" contained in the Fourteenth Amendment. In other words, all of the justices agree that punishments must be implemented under the Constitution's requirements for fairness and equity. They do not agree, however, on

3. "Death Row Appeals," *Akron Beacon Journal*, Mar. 20, 1990, p. A6.

which procedures meet constitutional standards for fairness. The final three cases reprinted in this chapter (*McCleskey v. Kemp, Murray v. Giarratano,* and *Butler v. McKellar*) demonstrate the justices' reactions when confronted with issues concerning fairness in the application of the death penalty.

In *McCleskey,* the Supreme Court considered sophisticated statistical evidence which revealed the existence of racial discrimination in death penalty sentencing. The *Murray* and *Butler* cases both involved habeas corpus petitions by death row inmates. After exhausting all appeals in the state courts, prisoners may, under a statute enacted by Congress, seek subsequent postconviction relief through habeas corpus petitions in the federal courts. In *Murray,* the Supreme Court addressed an assertion by indigent death row inmates that they were entitled to an appointed attorney to present their postconviction petitions. In *Butler,* the issue concerned retroactive application of Supreme Court decisions through habeas corpus claims. After Butler was sentenced to death, the Supreme Court decided in a separate case that the police used improper procedures by questioning a suspect in circumstances similar to Butler's. The question was whether Butler should benefit from a determination in a separate case that his rights had been violated by the procedures used by the police.

In all three cases, the issue of fairness in the application of the death penalty clashes with some justices' evident policy preference to maintain the states' ability to utilize capital punishment. In essence, by making the policy choice to maintain and expedite the application of capital punishment, a slim majority on the Court relaxed the application of Fourteenth Amendment fairness principles (i.e., "due process" and "equal protection") which might, if emphasized, threaten the continued existence of the death penalty.

ENMUND v. FLORIDA

458 U.S. 782 (1982)

Justice WHITE delivered the opinion of the Court [joined by Justices BRENNAN, MARSHALL, BLACKMUN, and STEVENS]:

I

The facts of this case, taken principally from the opinion of the Florida Supreme Court, are as follows. On April 1, 1975, at approximately 7:45 a.m., Thomas and Eunice Kersey, aged 86 and 74, were robbed and fatally shot at their farmhouse in central Florida. The evidence showed that

Sampson and Jeanette Armstrong had gone to the back door of the Kersey house and asked for water for an overheated car. When Mr. Kersey came out of the house, Sampson Armstrong grabbed him, pointed a gun at him, and told Jeanette Armstrong to take his money. Mr. Kersey cried for help, and his wife came out of the house with a gun and shot Jeanette Armstrong, wounding her. Sampson Armstrong, and perhaps Jeanette Armstrong, then shot and killed both of the Kerseys, dragged them into the kitchen, and took their money and fled.

Two witnesses testified that they drove past the Kersey house . . . and saw a large cream- or yellow-colored car parked beside the road about 200 yards from the house and that a man was sitting in the car. Another witness testified that . . . he saw Ida Jean Shaw, [Enmund's] common-law wife and Jeanette Armstrong's mother, driving a yellow Buick with a vinyl top which belonged to her and petitioner Earl Enmund. Enmund was a passenger in the car along with an unidentified woman. At about 8 a.m. the same witness saw the car return at a high rate of speed. Enmund was driving, Ida Jean Shaw was in the front seat, and one of the other two people in the car was lying down across the back seat. . . .

The jury found both Enmund and Sampson Armstrong guilty of first-degree murder and one count of robbery. . . . The trial judge then sentenced Enmund to death on the two counts of first-degree murder.
. . .

The Florida Supreme Court . . . rejected petitioner's argument that at most he could be found guilty of second-degree murder under Florida's felony-murder rule. The court explained that the interaction of the " 'felony murder rule and the law of principals combine to make a felon generally responsible for the lethal acts of his co-felon.' " . . .

. . . [T]he question [is] whether death is a valid penalty under the Eighth and Fourteenth Amendments for one who neither took life, attempted to take life, nor intended to take life.

II

. . . We have concluded that imposition of the death penalty in these circumstances is inconsistent with the Eighth and Fourteenth Amendments. . . .

. . . While the current legislative judgment [of the various states throughout the country] with respect to imposition of the death penalty where a defendant did not take life, attempt to take it, or intend to take life is neither "wholly unanimous among state legislatures," *Coker v. Georgia,* . . . nor as compelling as the legislative judgments considered in *Coker* [to reject capital punishment for rape], it nevertheless weighs on the side of rejecting capital punishment for the crime at issue. . . .

III

. . . .

Here the robbers did commit murder; but they were subjected to the death penalty only because they killed as well as robbed. The question before us is not the disproportionality of death as a penalty for murder, but rather the validity of capital punishment for Enmund's own conduct. The focus must be on *his* culpability, not on that of those who committed the robbery and shot victims. . . . Enmund himself did not kill or attempt to kill; and, as construed by the Florida Supreme Court, the record before us does not warrant a finding that Enmund had any intention of participating in or facilitating a murder. Yet under Florida law death was an authorized penalty because Enmund aided and abetted a robbery in the course of which murder was committed. It is fundamental that "causing harm intentionally must be punished more severely than causing the same harm unintentionally." . . . Enmund did not kill or intend to kill and thus his culpability is plainly different from that of the robbers who killed; yet the State treated them alike and attributed to Enmund the culpability of those who killed the Kerseys. This was impermissible under the Eighth Amendment. . . .

For purposes of imposing the death penalty, Enmund's criminal culpability must be limited to his participation in the robbery, and his punishment must be tailored to his personal responsibility and moral guilt. Putting Enmund to death to avenge two killings that he did not commit and had no intention of committing or causing does not measurably contribute to the retributive end of ensuring that the criminal gets his just desserts. . . .

Justice O'CONNER dissenting [joined by Chief Justice BURGER and Justices POWELL and REHNQUIST]:

. . . I dissent from this holding not only because I believe that it is not supported by the analysis in our previous cases, but also because today's holding interferes with state criteria for assessing legal guilt by recasting intent as a matter of constitutional law. . . .

Although the Court disingenuously seeks to characterize Enmund as only a "robber," . . . it cannot be disputed that he is responsible, along with Sampson and Jeanette Armstrong, for the murders of the Kerseys. There is no dispute that their lives were unjustifiably taken, and that the petitioner, as one who aided and abetted the armed robbery, is legally liable for their deaths. . . .

TISON v. ARIZONA

481 U.S. 137 (1987)

Justice O'CONNOR delivered the opinion of the Court [joined by Chief Justice REHNQUIST and Justices WHITE, POWELL, and SCALIA]:

The question presented is whether petitioners' participation in the events leading up to and following the murder of four members of a family makes the sentences of death imposed by the Arizona courts constitutionally permissible although neither petitioner specifically intended to kill the victims and neither inflicted the fatal gunshot wounds. We hold that the Arizona Supreme Court applied an erroneous standard in making the findings required by *Enmund v. Florida* ... and, therefore, vacate the judgments below and remand the case for further proceedings not inconsistent with this opinion.

I

Gary Tison was sentenced to life imprisonment as the result of a prison escape during the course of which he had killed a guard. After he had been in prison a number of years, Gary Tison's wife, their three sons Donald, Ricky, and Raymond, Gary's brother Joseph, and other relatives made plans to help Gary Tison escape again. ... The Tison family assembled a large arsenal of weapons for this purpose. Plans for escape were discussed with Gary Tison, who insisted that his cellmate, Randy Greenawalt, also a convicted murderer, be included in the prison break. The following facts are largely evidenced by petitioners' detailed confessions given as part of a plea bargain according to the terms of which the State agreed not to seek the death sentence. The Arizona courts interpreted the plea agreement to require that petitioners testify to the planning stages of the breakout. When they refused to do so, the bargain was rescinded and they were tried, convicted, and sentenced to death.

On July 30, 1978, the three Tison brothers entered the Arizona State Prison at Florence carrying a large ice chest filled with guns. The Tisons armed Greenawalt and their father, and the group, brandishing their weapons, locked the prison guards and visitors present in a storage closet. The five men fled the prison grounds in the Tisons' Ford Galaxy automobile. No shots were fired at the prison.

After leaving the prison, the men abandoned the Ford automobile and proceeded on to an isolated house in a white Lincoln automobile that the brothers had parked at a hospital near the prison. At the house, the Lincoln automobile had a flat tire; the only spare tire was pressed into service. After two nights at the house, the group drove towards Flagstaff. As the group traveled on back roads and secondary highways through the desert, another tire blew out. The group decided to flag down a passing motorist and steal a car. Raymond stood out in front of the Lincoln; the other four armed themselves and laid in wait by the side of the road. One car passed by without stopping, but a second car, a Mazda occupied by John Lyons, his wife Donnelda, his 2-year-old son Christopher and his 15-year-old niece, Theresa Tyson, pulled over to render aid.

As Raymond showed John Lyons the flat tire on the Lincoln, the other Tisons and Greenawalt emerged. The Lyons family was forced into the backseat of the Lincoln. Raymond and Donald drove the Lincoln down a dirt road off the highway and then down a gas line service road farther into the desert; Gary Tison, Ricky Tison and Randy Greenawalt followed in the Lyons' Mazda. The two cars were parked trunk to trunk and Lyons family was ordered to stand in front of the Lincoln's headlights. The Tisons transferred their belongings from the Lincoln into the Mazda. They discovered guns and money in the Mazda which they kept and they put the rest of the Lyons' possessions in the Lincoln.

Gary Tison then told Raymond to drive the Lincoln still farther into the desert. Raymond did so, and, while the others guarded the Lyons and Theresa Tyson, Gary fired his shotgun into the radiator, presumably to disable the vehicle. The Lyons and Theresa Tyson were then escorted to the Lincoln and again ordered to stand in its headlights. Ricky Tison reported that John Lyons begged, in comments "more or less directed at everybody," "Jesus, don't kill me." Gary Tison said he was "thinking about it." . . . John Lyons asked the Tisons and Greenawalt to "[g]ive us some water . . . just leave us out here, and you all go home." Gary Tison then told his sons to go back to the Mazda and get some water. Raymond later explained that his father "was like in conflict with himself . . . [w]hat it was, I think it was the baby being there and all this, and he wasn't sure about what to do." . . .

The petitioners' statements diverge to some extent, but it appears that both of them went back towards the Mazda, along with Donald, while Randy Greenawalt and Gary Tison stayed at the Lincoln guarding the victims. Raymond recalled being at the Mazda filling the water jug "when we started hearing the shots." . . . Ricky said that the brothers gave the water jug to Gary Tison who then, with Randy Greenawalt went behind the Lincoln, where they spoke briefly, then raised the shotguns and started firing. . . . In any event, petitioners agree they saw Greenawalt and their father brutally murder their four captives with repeated blasts from their shotguns. Neither made an effort to help the victims, though both later stated they were surprised by the shooting. The Tisons got into the

Mazda and drove away, continuing their flight. Physical evidence suggested that Theresa Tyson managed to crawl away from the bloodbath, severely injured. She died in the desert after the Tisons left.

Several days later the Tisons and Greenawalt were apprehended after a shootout at a police roadblock. Donald Tison was killed. Gary Tison escaped into the desert where he subsequently died of exposure. Raymond and Ricky Tison and Randy Greenawalt were captured and tried jointly for the crimes associated with the prison break itself and the shootout at the roadblock; each was convicted and sentenced.

The State then individually tried each of the petitioners for capital murder of the four victims as well as for the associated crimes of armed robbery, kidnapping, and car theft. The capital murder charges were based on Arizona felony-murder law providing that a killing occurring during the perpetration of robbery or kidnapping is capital murder, . . . and that each participant in the kidnapping or robbery is legally responsible for the acts of his accomplices. Each of the petitioners was convicted of the four murders under these accomplice liability and felony-murder statutes. . . .

. . . [T]he judge sentenced both petitioners to death. . . .

II

In *Enmund v. Florida*, . . . this Court reversed the death sentence of a defendant convicted under Florida's felony-murder rule. Enmund was the driver of a "get-away" car in an armed robbery of a dwelling. The occupants of the house, an elderly couple, resisted and Enmund's accomplices killed them. . . .

This Court, citing the weight of legislative and community opinion, found a broad societal consensus, with which it agreed, that the death penalty was disproportional to the crime of robbery-felony murder "in these circumstances." . . .

After surveying the States' felony-murder statutes, the *Enmund* Court next examined the behavior of juries in cases like Enmund's in its attempt to assess American attitudes towards capital punishment in felony-murder cases. Of 739 death row inmates, only 41 did not participate in the fatal assault. All but 16 of these were physically present at the scene of the murder and of these only 3, including Enmund, were sentenced to death in the absence of a finding that they had collaborated in a scheme designed to kill. The court found the fact that only 3 of 739 death row inmates had been sentenced to death absent an intent to kill, physical presence or direct participation in the fatal assault persuasive evidence that American juries considered the death sentence disproportional to felony-murder simpliciter. . . .

... Furthermore, the Court found that Enmund's degree of participation in *the murders* was so tangential that it could not be said to justify a sentence of death. . . .

... Since Enmund's own participation in the felony murder was so attenuated and since there was no proof that Enmund had any culpable mental state, . . . the death penalty was excessive retribution for his crimes. . . .

[The Tisons] argue strenuously that they did not "intend to kill" as that concept has been generally understood in the common law. We accept this as true. . . . As petitioners point out, there is no evidence that either Ricky or Raymond Tison took any act which he desired to, or was substantially certain would, cause death. . . .

... [I]t is equally clear that petitioners also fall outside the category of felony murders for whom *Enmund* explicitly held the death penalty disproportional: their degree of participation in the crimes was major rather than minor, and the record would support a finding of the culpable mental state of reckless indifference to human life. . . .

Raymond Tison brought an arsenal of lethal weapons into the Arizona State Prison which he then handed over to two convicted murderers, one of whom he knew had killed a guard in the course of a previous escape attempt. By his own admission he was prepared to kill in furtherance of the prison break. He performed the crucial role of flagging down a passing car occupied by an innocent family whose fate was then entrusted to the known killers he had previously armed. He robbed these people at their direction and then guarded the victims at gunpoint while they considered what next to do. He stood by and watched the killing, making no effort to assist the victims before, during, or after the shooting. Instead, he chose to assist the killers in their continuing criminal endeavors, ending in a gun battle with the police in the final showdown.

Ricky Tison's behavior differs in slight details only. Like Raymond, he intentionally brought the guns into the prison to arm the murderers. He could have foreseen that lethal force might be used, particularly since he knew that his father's previous escape attempt had resulted in murder. He, too, participated fully in the kidnapping and robbery and watched the killing after which he chose to aid those whom he had placed in the position to kill rather than their victims.

These facts not only indicate that the Tison brothers' participation in the crime was anything but minor, they also would clearly support a finding that they both subjectively appreciated that their acts were likely to result in the taking of innocent life. The issue raised by this case is whether the Eighth Amendment prohibits the death penalty in the intermediate case of the defendant whose participation is major and whose mental state is one of reckless indifference to the value of human life. *Enmund* does not specifically address this point. . . .

A critical facet of the individualized determination of culpability required in capital cases is the mental state with which the defendant commits the crime. Deeply ingrained in our legal tradition is the idea that the more purposeful is the criminal conduct, the more serious is the offense, and, therefore, the more severely it ought to be punished. . . .

. . . [S]ome nonintentional murderers may be among the most dangerous and inhumane of all—the person who tortures another not caring whether the victim lives or dies, or the robber who shoots someone in the course of the robbery, utterly indifferent to the fact that the desire to rob may have the unintended consequence of killing the victim as well as taking the victim's property. This reckless indifference to the value of human life may be every bit as shocking to the moral sense as an "intent to kill." . . . *Enmund* held that when "intent to kill" results in its logical though not inevitable consequence—the taking of human life— the Eighth Amendment permits the State to exact the death penalty after a careful weighing of the aggravating and mitigating circumstances. Similarly, we hold that the reckless disregard for human life implicit in knowingly engaging in criminal activities known to carry a grave risk of death represents a highly culpable mental state, a mental state that may be taken into account in making a capital sentencing judgment when that conduct causes its natural, though also not inevitable, lethal result. . . .

. . . [W]e simply hold that major participation in the felony committed, combined with reckless indifference to human life, is sufficient to satisfy the *Enmund* culpability requirement. The Arizona courts have clearly found that the former exists [as regards the Tison brothers]; we now vacate the judgments and remand for determination of the latter [element of reckless indifference to human life]. . . .

Justice BRENNAN dissented [joined by Justices MARSHALL, BLACK-MUN, and STEVENS]:

The murders that Gary Tison and Randy Greenawalt committed revolt and grieve all who learn of them. When the deaths of the Lyons family and Theresa Tyson were first reported, many in Arizona erupted "in a towering yell" for retribution and justice [according to the *Arizona Republic* newspaper]. Yet Gary Tison, the central figure in this tragedy, the man who had his family arrange his and Greenawalt's escape from prison, and the man who chose, with Greenawalt, to murder this family while his sons stood by, died of exposure in the desert before society could arrest him and bring him to trial. The question this case presents is what punishment Arizona may constitutionally exact from two of Gary Tison's sons for their role in these events. Because our precedents and our Constitution compel a different answer than the one the Court reaches today, I dissent.

I

. . . [T]he felony-murder doctrine . . . is a living fossil from a legal era in which all felonies were punishable by death; in those circumstances, the state of mind of the felon with respect to the murder was understandably superfluous, because he or she could be executed simply for intentionally committing the felony. Today, in most American jurisdictions and in virtually all European and Commonwealth countries, a felon cannot be executed for a murder that he or she did not commit or specifically intend or attempt to commit. In some American jurisdictions, however, the authority to impose death in such circumstances still persists. Arizona is such a jurisdiction. . . .

. . . [W]hile the Arizona courts acknowledged that petitioners had neither participated in the shootings nor intended that they occur, those courts nonetheless imposed the death sentence under the theory of felony murder. . . .

. . . [In *Enmund*], the Court . . . explained, and rejected, the felony-murder doctrine as a theory of capital culpability. . . .

Enmund obviously casts considerable doubt on the constitutionality of the death sentences imposed on [the Tisons]. . . .

The Court has chosen . . . to announce a new substantive standard for capital liability: a defendant's "major participation in the felony committed, combined with reckless indifference to human life, is sufficient to satisfy the *Enmund* culpability requirement." . . . The Court then remands the case for a determination by the state court whether the petitioners are culpable under this new standard. Nevertheless, the Court observes, in dictum, that "the record would support a finding of the culpable mental state of reckless indifference to human life." . . .

I join no part of this. First, the Court's dictum that its new category of *mens rea* is applicable to these petitioners is not supported by the record. Second, even assuming petitioners may be so categorized, objective evidence and this Court's Eighth Amendment jurisprudence demonstrate that the death penalty is disproportionate punishment for this category of defendants. Finally, the fact that the Court reaches a different conclusion is illustrative of the profound problems that continue to plague capital sentencing.

II

The facts on which the Court relies are not sufficient, in my view, to support the Court's conclusion that petitioners acted with reckless disregard for human life.[4] . . .

. . . While the Court states that petitioners were on the scene during the shooting and that they watched it occur, Raymond stated that he and Ricky were still engaged in repacking the Mazda after finding the water jug when the shootings occurred. . . . Ricky stated that they had returned with the water, but were still some distance ("farther than this room") from the Lincoln when the shootings started, . . . and that the brothers then turned away from the scene and went back to the Mazda. . . . Neither stated that they anticipated that the shootings would occur, or that they could have done anything to prevent them or to help the victims afterward.[6] Both, however, expressed feelings of surprise, helplessness, and regret. This statement of Raymond's is illustrative:

> "Well, I just think you should know when we first came into this we had an agreement with my dad that nobody would get hurt because we [the brothers] wanted no one hurt. And when this [killing of the kidnap victims] came about we were not expecting it. And it took us by surprise as much as it took the family [the victims] by surprise because we were not expecting this to happen. And I feel bad about it happening. I wish we could [have done] something to stop it, but by

---

4. Petitioners' presence at the scene of the murders, and their participation in flagging down the vehicle, and robbing and guarding the family, indicate nothing whatsoever about their subjective appreciation that their father and his friend would suddenly decide to kill the family. Each of the petitioners' actions was perfectly consistent with, and indeed necessary to, the felony of stealing a car in order to continue the flight from prison. Nothing in the record suggests that any of their actions were inconsistent with that aim. . . . Thus the Court's findings about petitioners' mental states regarding the murders are based solely on inferences from petitioners' participation in the underlying felonies. Their decision to provide arms for and participate in a prison breakout and escape may support the lower court's finding that they should have anticipated that lethal force might be used during the breakout and subsequent flight, but it does not support the Court's conclusions about petitioners' mental states concerning the shootings that actually occurred.

5. [Omitted.]

6. In addition, the Court's statement that Raymond did not act to assist the victims "after" the shooting, and its statement that Ricky "watched the killing after which he chose to aid those whom he placed in the position to kill rather than their victims," . . . takes license with the facts found by the Arizona Supreme Court. That court did not say whether petitioners did anything to help the victims following the shooting, nor did it make any findings that would lead one to believe that something could have been done to assist them. The lower court merely stated that petitioners did not "disassociate" themselves from their father and Greenawalt after the shooting. . . .

the time it happened it was too late to stop it. And it's just something we are going to live with the rest of our lives. It will always be there."[7]

... The discrepancy between those aspects of the record on which the Court has chosen to focus and those aspects it has chosen to ignore underscores the point that a reliable individualized *Enmund* determination can be made only by the trial court following an evidentiary hearing. ...

III

... [T]he basic flaw in today's decision is the Court's failure to conduct the sort of proportionality analysis that the Constitution and past cases require. Creation of a new category of culpability is not enough to distinguish this case from *Enmund*. ... In other words, the Court must demonstrate that major participation in a felony with a state of mind of reckless indifference to human life deserves the same punishment as intending to commit a murder or actually committing a murder. ...

... [T]his case, like *Enmund*, involves accomplices *who did not kill*. Thus, although some of the "most culpable and dangerous murderers" may be those who kill without specifically intending to kill, it is considerably more difficult to apply that rubric convincingly to those who not only did not intend to kill, but who also have not killed.

It is precisely in this context—where the defendant has not killed—that a finding that he or she nevertheless intended to kill seems indispensable to establishing capital culpability. It is important first to note that

---

7. These expressions are consistent with other evidence about the sons' mental states that this Court, like the lower courts, has neglected. ... Both lived at home with their mother, and visited their father, whom they believed to be "a model prisoner," each week. ... They did not plan the breakout or escape; rather their father after thinking about it himself for a year, mentioned the idea to Raymond for the first time one week before the breakout, and discussed with his sons the possibility of having them participate only the day before the breakout. ... The sons conditioned their participation on their father's promise that no one would get hurt; during the breakout, their father kept his word. ... Given these circumstances, the sons' own testimony that they were surprised by the killings, and did not expect them to occur, appears more plausible than the Court's speculation that they "subjectively appreciated that their activities were likely to result in the taking of innocent life." The report of the psychologist, who examined both sons, also suggests that they may not have appreciated the consequences of their participation:

"These most unfortunate youngsters were born into an extremely pathological family and were exposed to one of the premier sociopaths of recent Arizona history. ... I do believe their father, Gary Tison, exerted a strong, consistent, destructive but subtle pressure upon these youngsters and I believe that these young men got committed to an act which was essentially 'over their heads.' ... "

such a defendant has not committed an *act* for which he or she could be sentenced to death. The applicability of the death penalty therefore turns entirely on the defendant's mental state with regard to an act committed by another. . . .

. . . The reckless actor has not *chosen* to bring about the killing in the way the intentional actor has. The person who chooses to act recklessly and is indifferent to the possibility of fatal consequences often deserves serious punishment. But because that person has not chosen to kill, his or her moral and criminal culpability is of a different degree than that of one who killed or intended to kill. . . .

IV

. . . .

. . . The urge to employ the felony-murder doctrine against accomplices is undoubtedly strong when the killings stir public passion and the actual murderer is beyond human grasp. An intuition that sons and daughters must sometimes be punished for the sins of the father may be deeply rooted in our consciousness. Yet punishment that conforms more closely to such retributive instincts than to the Eighth Amendment is tragically anachronistic in a society governed by our Constitution.

. . . The persistence of doctrines (such as felony murder) that allow excessive discretion in apportioning criminal culpability, and of decisions (such as today's) that do not even attempt "precisely [to] delineate the particular types of conduct and states of mind warranting imposition of the death penalty," . . . demonstrate that this Court still has not articulated rules that will ensure that capital sentencing decisions conform to the substantive principles of the Eighth Amendment. Arbitrariness continues so to infect both the procedure and substance of capital sentencing that any decision to impose the death penalty remains cruel and unusual punishment. . . . I adhere to my view that the death penalty is in all circumstances cruel and unusual punishment prohibited by the Eighth and Fourteenth Amendments, and dissent.

McCLESKEY v. KEMP

481 U.S. 278 (1987)

Justice POWELL delivered the opinion of the Court [joined by Chief Justice REHNQUIST and Justices WHITE, O'CONNOR, and SCALIA]:

This case presents the question whether a complex statistical study that indicates a risk that racial considerations enter into capital sentencing determinations proves that petitioner McCleskey's capital sentence is unconstitutional under the Eighth or Fourteenth Amendment.

I

McCleskey, a black man, was convicted of two counts of armed robbery and one count of murder in the Superior Court of Fulton County, Georgia, on October 12, 1978. . . . During the course of [a furniture store] robbery, a police officer, answering a silent alarm, entered the store through the front door. As he was walking down the center aisle of the store, two shots were fired. Both struck the officer. One hit him in the face and killed him.

Several weeks later, McCleskey was arrested in connection with an unrelated offense. He confessed that he participated in the furniture store robbery, but denied that he had shot the police officer. At trial, the State introduced evidence that at least one of the bullets that struck the officer was fired from a .38 caliber Rossi revolver. This description matched the description of the gun that McCleskey had carried during the robbery. The State also introduced the testimony of two witnesses who had heard McCleskey admit to the shooting.

The jury convicted McCleskey of murder. . . . The jury recommended that he be sentenced to death on the murder charge and to consecutive life sentences on the armed robbery charges. The court followed the jury's recommendation and sentenced McCleskey to death. . . .

McCleskey . . . filed a petition for a writ of habeas corpus in [federal court]. . . . His petition raised 18 claims, one of which was that the Georgia capital sentencing process is administered in a racially discriminatory manner in violation of the Eighth and Fourteenth Amendments to the United States Constitution. In support of his claim, McCleskey proffered a statistical study performed by Professors David C. Baldus, George Woodworth, and Charles Pulaski (the Baldus study) that purports to show disparity in the imposition of the death sentence in Georgia based on the race of the murder victim and, to a lesser extent, the race of the defendant. The Baldus study is actually two sophisticated statistical studies that examine over 2,000 murder cases that occurred in Georgia during the 1970s. The raw numbers collected by Professor Baldus indicate that defendants charged with killing white persons received the death penalty in 11% of cases, but defendants charged with killing blacks received the death penalty in only 1% of cases. The raw numbers also indicate a reverse disparity according to the race of the defendant: 4% of the black defendants received the death penalty, as opposed to 7% of the white defendants.

Baldus also divided the cases according to the combination of the race of the defendant and the race of the victim. He found that the death penalty was assessed in 22% of the cases involving black defendants and white victims; 8% of the cases involving white defendants and white victims; 1% of the cases involving black defendants and black victims; and 3% of the cases involving white defendants and black victims. Similarly, Baldus found that prosecutors sought the death penalty in 70% of the cases involving black defendants and white victims; 32% of the cases involving white defendants and white victims; 15% of the cases involving black defendants and black victims; and 19% of the cases involving white defendants and black victims.

Baldus subjected his data to an extensive analysis, taking account of 230 variables that could have explained the disparities on nonracial grounds. One of his models concludes that, even after taking account of 39 nonracial variables, defendants charged with killing white victims were 4.3 times as likely to receive a death sentence as defendants charged with killing blacks. According to this model, black defendants were 1.1 times as likely to receive a death sentence as other defendants. Thus, the Baldus study indicates that black defendants, such as Mc-Cleskey, who kill white victims have the greatest likelihood of receiving the death penalty.[5]

The District Court . . . concluded that McCleskey's "statistics do not demonstrate a prima facie case in support of the contention that the death penalty was imposed upon him because of his race, because of the race of the victim, or because of any Eighth Amendment concern." . . . As to McCleskey's Fourteenth Amendment claim, the court found that the methodology of the Baldus study was flawed in several respects.[6] . . .

---

5. Baldus's 230-variable model divided cases into eight different ranges, according to the estimated aggravation level of the offense. Baldus argued in his testimony to the District Court that the effects of racial bias were most striking in the mid-range cases. "[W]hen the cases become tremendously aggravated so that everybody would agree that if we're going to have a death sentence, these are the cases that should get it, the race effects go away. It's only in the mid-range of cases where the decision makers have a real choice as to what to do. If there's room for the exercise of discretion, then [racial] factors begin to play a role." . . . Under this model, Baldus found that 14.4% of the black-victim mid-range cases received the death penalty, and 34.4% of the white-victim cases received the death penalty. . . . According to Baldus, the facts of McCleskey's case placed it within the mid-range.

6. [T]he District Court noted that in many respects the data were incomplete. In its view, the questionnaires used to obtain the data failed to capture the full degree of the aggravating or mitigating circumstances. . . . The Court criticized the researcher's decisions regarding unknown variables. . . .

II

... As a black defendant who killed a white victim, McCleskey claims that the Baldus study demonstrates that he was discriminated against because of the race of his victim. In its broadest form, McCleskey's claim of discrimination extends to every actor in the Georgia capital sentencing process, from the prosecutor who sought the death penalty and the jury that imposed the sentence, to the State itself that enacted the capital punishment statute and allows it to remain in effect despite its allegedly discriminatory application. We agree with the [lower courts] . . . that this claim must fail.

... [T]o prevail under the Equal Protection Clause, McCleskey must prove that the decisionmakers in *his* case acted with discriminatory purpose. He offers no evidence specific to his own case that would support an inference that racial considerations played a part in his sentence. Instead, he relies solely on the Baldus study. McCleskey argues that the Baldus study compels an inference that his sentence rests on purposeful discrimination. . . .

This Court has accepted statistics as proof of intent to discriminate in certain limited contexts. First, this Court has accepted statistical disparities as proof of an equal protection violation in the selection of the jury venire in a particular district. . . . Second, this Court has accepted statistics in the form of multiple regression analysis to prove statutory violations under Title VII [regarding employment discrimination]. . . .

But the nature of capital sentencing decision, and the relationship of the statistics to that decision, are fundamentally different from the corresponding elements in the venire-selection or Title VII cases. Most importantly, each particular decision to impose the death penalty is made by a petit jury selected from a properly constituted venire. Each jury is unique in its composition, and the Constitution requires that its decision rest on consideration of innumerable factors that vary according to the characteristics of the individual defendant and the facts of the particular capital offense. . . . Thus, the application of an inference drawn from the general statistics to a specific decision in a trial and sentencing simply is not comparable to the application of an inference drawn from general statistics to a specific venire-selection or Title VII case. In those cases, the statistics relate to fewer entities, and fewer variables are relevant to the challenged decisions.

Another important difference between the cases in which we have accepted statistics as proof of discriminatory intent and this case is that, in the venire-selection and Title II contexts, the decisionmaker has an opportunity to explain the statistical disparity. . . .

Finally, McCleskey's statistical proffer must be viewed in the context

of his challenge ... at the heart of the State's criminal justice system. ...
Implementation of [criminal justice] laws necessarily requires discretionary judgments. Because discretion is essential to the criminal justice process, we would demand exceptionally clear proof before we would infer
that the discretion has been abused. ... [W]e hold that the Baldus study is
clearly insufficient to support an inference that any of the decisionmakers in McCleskey's case acted with discriminatory purpose. ...

... As legislatures necessarily have wide discretion in the choice of
criminal laws and penalties, and as there were legitimate reasons for the
Georgia Legislature to adopt and maintain capital punishment, ... we
will not infer a discriminatory purpose on the part of the State of Georgia.
...

IV

... McCleskey argues that the sentence in his case is disproportionate to
the sentences in other murder cases. ...

... [A]bsent a showing that the Georgia capital punishment system
operates in an arbitrary and capricious manner, McCleskey cannot prove
a constitutional violation by demonstrating that other defendants who
may be similarly situated did *not* receive the death penalty. ...

Because McCleskey's sentence was imposed under Georgia sentencing procedures that focus discretion "on the particularized nature of the
crime and the particularized characteristics of the individual defendant,"
... we lawfully may presume that McClesky's death sentence was not
"wantonly and freakishly" imposed, ... and thus that the sentence is not
disproportionate within any recognized meaning under the Eighth
Amendment.

... [M]cCleskey further contends that the Georgia capital punishment system is arbitrary and capricious in *application*, and therefore his
sentence is excessive, because racial considerations may influence capital
sentencing decisions in Georgia. ...

... Even Professor Baldus does not contend that his statistics *prove*
that race enters into any capital sentencing decisions or that race was a
factor in McCleskey's particular case. Statistics at most show only a likelihood that a particular factor entered into some decisions. There is, of
course, some risk of racial prejudice influencing a jury's decision in a
criminal case. There are similar risks that other kinds of prejudice will influence other criminal trials. ... The question is "at what point that risk
becomes constitutionally unacceptable." ... McCleskey asks us to accept
the likelihood allegedly shown by the Baldus study as the constitutional
measure of unacceptable risk of racial prejudice influencing capital sentencing decisions. This we decline to do. ...

McCleskey's argument that the Constitution condemns the discretion allowed decisionmakers in the Georgia capital sentencing system is antithetical to the fundamental role of discretion in our criminal justice system. Discretion in the criminal justice system offers substantial benefits to the criminal defendant. Not only can a jury decline to impose the death sentence, it can decline to convict. . . .

At most, the Baldus study indicates a discrepancy that appears to correlate with race. Apparent disparities in sentencing are an inevitable part of our criminal justice system. . . .

V

. . . McCleskey's claim, taken to its logical conclusion, throws into serious question the principles that underlie our entire criminal justice system. The Eighth Amendment is not limited in application to capital punishment, but applies to all penalties. . . . Thus, if we accepted McCleskey's claim that racial bias has impermissibly tainted the capital sentencing decision, we could soon be faced with similar claims as to other types of penalty. . . .

. . . McCleskey's arguments are best presented to legislative bodies. . . . Legislatures . . . are better qualified to weigh and "evaluate the results of statistical studies in terms of their own local conditions." . . .

Justice BRENNAN dissenting [joined by Justice MARSHALL; Justices BLACKMUN and STEVENS joined in all but Part I]:

I

. . . [M]urder defendants in Georgia with white victims are more than four times as likely to receive the death sentence as are defendants with black victims. . . . Nothing could convey more powerfully the intractable reality of the death penalty: "that the effort to eliminate arbitrariness in the infliction of that ultimate sanction is so plainly doomed to failure that it— and the death penalty—must be abandoned altogether." . . .

II

At some point in this case, Warren McCleskey doubtless asked his lawyer whether a jury was likely to sentence him to die. A candid reply to this question would have been disturbing. First, counsel would have to tell McCleskey that few of the details of the crime or of McCleskey's past criminal conduct were more important than the fact that his victim was white. . . . Furthermore, counsel would feel bound to tell McCleskey that defendants charged with killing white victims in Georgia are 4.3 times as likely to be sentenced to death as defendants charged with killing blacks. . . . In addition, frankness would compel the disclosure that it was more likely than not that the race of McCleskey's victim would determine whether he received a death sentence: 6 of every 11 defendants convicted of killing a white person would not have received the death penalty if their victims had been black. . . .

The Court today . . . finds no fault in a system in which lawyers must tell their clients that race casts a large shadow on the capital sentencing process. The Court arrives at this conclusion by stating that the Baldus study cannot *"prove* that race enters into any capital sentencing decisions." . . . [W]e can identify only "a likelihood that a particular factor entered into some decisions," . . . and "a discrepancy that appears to correlate to race." . . . This "likelihood" and "discrepancy," holds the Court, is insufficient to establish a constitutional violation. The Court reaches this conclusion by placing four factors on the scales opposite McCleskey's evidence: the desire to encourage sentencing discretion, the existence of "statutory safeguards" in the Georgia scheme, the fear of encouraging widespread challenges to other sentencing decisions, and the limits of the judicial role. The Court's evaluation of the significance of petitioner's evidence is fundamentally at odds with our consistent concern for rationality in capital sentencing, and the considerations that the majority invokes to discount that evidence cannot justify its force.

III

It is important to emphasize at the outset that the Court's observation that McCleskey cannot prove the influence of race on any particular sentencing decision is irrelevant in evaluating his Eighth Amendment claim. Since *Furman v. Georgia* [1972], . . . the court has been concerned with the *risk* of the imposition of an arbitrary sentence, rather than the proven fact of one. *Furman* held that the death penalty "may not be imposed under sentencing procedures that create a substantial risk that the punishment will be inflicted in an arbitrary and capricious manner." . . .

Defendants challenging their death sentences thus never have had to prove that impermissible considerations have actually infected sentencing decisions. We have required instead that they establish that the system under which they were sentenced posed a significant risk of such an occurrence. McCleskey's claim does differ, however, in one respect from these earlier cases: it is the first to base a challenge not on speculation about how a system *might* operate, but empirical documentation of how it *does* operate.

The Court assumes the statistical validity of the Baldus study, . . . and

acknowledges that McCleskey has demonstrated a risk that racial prejudice plays a role in capital sentencing in Georgia. . . . Nevertheless, it finds
the probability of prejudice insufficient to create constitutional concern.
. . . Close analysis of the Baldus study, however, in light of both statistical
principles and human experience, reveals that the risk that race influenced McCleskey's sentence is intolerable by any imaginable standard. . . .

. . . [B]lacks who kill whites are sentenced to death at nearly 22 *times* the
rate of blacks who kill blacks, and more than 7 *times* the rate of whites who
kill blacks. . . . Since our decision upholding the Georgia capital-sentencing
system in *Gregg,* the State has executed 7 persons. All of the 7 were executed
for killing whites, and 6 of the 7 executed were black. Such execution figures
are especially striking in light of the fact that, during the period encompassed
by the Baldus study, only 9.2% of Georgia homicides involved black defendants and white victims, while 60.7% involved black victims.

McCleskey's statistics have particular force because most of them
are the product of sophisticated multiple-regression analysis. Such analysis is designed precisely to identify patterns in the aggregate, even though
we may not be able to reconstitute with certainty any individual decision
that goes to make up that pattern. Multiple-regression analysis is particularly well-suited to identify the influence of impermissible considerations
in sentencing, since it is able to control for permissible factors that may
explain an apparent arbitrary pattern. . . . In this case, Professor Baldus in
fact conducted additional regression analyses in response to criticisms
and suggestions by the District Court, all of which confirmed, and some
of which even strengthened, the study's original conclusions.

The statistical evidence in this case thus relentlessly documents the
risk that McCleskey's sentence was influenced by racial considerations.
. . .

. . . We must also ask whether the conclusion suggested by those numbers [in the Baldus study] is consonant with our understanding of history
and human experience. Georgia's legacy of a race-conscious criminal justice system, as well as this Court's own recognition of the persistent danger
that racial attitudes may affect criminal proceedings, indicate that Mc-
Cleskey's claim is not a fanciful product of mere statistical artifice. . . .

IV

. . . .

The Court maintains that petitioner's claim "is antithetical to the fundamental role of discretion in our criminal justice system." . . .

Reliance on race in imposing capital punishment, however, is antithetical to the very rationale for granting sentencing discretion. Discretion is a means, not an end. It is bestowed in order to permit the sentencer

to "trea[t] each defendant in a capital case with that degree of respect due the uniqueness of the individual." . . .

Considering the race of the defendant or victim in deciding if the death penalty should be imposed is completely at odds with this concern that an individual be evaluated as a unique human being. . . . Enhanced willingness to impose the death sentence on black defendants, or diminished willingness to render such a sentence when blacks are victims, reflects a devaluation of the lives of black persons. . . .

The Court . . . states that its unwillingness to regard the petitioner's evidence as sufficient is based in part on the fear that recognition of McCleskey's claim would open the door to widespread challenges to all aspects of criminal sentencing. . . . Taken on its face, such a statement seems to suggest a fear of too much justice. Yet surely the majority would acknowledge that if striking evidence indicated that other minority groups, or women, or even persons with blond hair, were disproportionately sentenced to death, such a state of affairs would be repugnant to deeply rooted conceptions of fairness. . . .

Justice BLACKMUN dissenting [joined by Justices BRENNAN, MARSHALL, and STEVENS]:

. . . .

IV

One of the final concerns discussed by the Court may be the most disturbing aspect of its opinion. Granting relief to McCleskey in this case, it is said, could lead to further constitutional challenges. . . . That, of course, is no reason to deny McCleskey his rights under the Equal Protection Clause. If a grant of relief to him were to lead to a closer examination of the effects of racial considerations throughout the criminal-justice system, the system, and hence society, might benefit. Where no such factors come into play, the integrity of the system is enhanced. Where such considerations are shown to be significant, efforts can be made to eradicate their impermissible influence and to ensure an evenhanded application of criminal sanctions. . . .

Justice STEVENS dissenting [joined by Justice BLACKMUN]:

. . . .

The Court's decision appears to be based on a fear that the acceptance of McCleskey's claim would sound the death knell for capital punishment in

Georgia. If society were indeed forced to choose between a racially discriminatory death penalty (one that provides heightened protection against murder "for whites only") and no death penalty at all, the choice mandated by the Constitution would be plain. . . . But the Court's fear is unfounded. One of the lessons of the Baldus study is that there exist certain categories of extremely serious crimes for which prosecutors consistently seek, and juries consistently impose, the death penalty without regard to the race of the victim or the race of the offender. If Georgia were to narrow the class of death-eligible defendants to those categories, the danger of arbitrary and discriminatory imposition of the death penalty would be significantly decreased, if not eradicated. As Justice BRENNAN has demonstrated in his dissenting opinion, such a restructuring of the sentencing scheme is surely not too high a price to pay.

MURRAY v. GIARRATANO

109 S. Ct. 2765 (1989)

Chief Justice REHNQUIST announced the judgment of the Court and delivered an opinion in which Justices WHITE, O'CONNOR, and SCALIA join [Justice KENNEDY concurred in the judgment]:

Virginia death row inmates brought a civil rights suit against various officials of the Commonwealth of Virginia. The prisoners claimed, based on several theories, that the Constitution required that they be provided with counsel at the State's expense for the purpose of pursuing collateral proceedings related to their convictions and sentences. The courts below ruled that appointment of counsel upon request was necessary for the prisoners to enjoy their constitutional right to access to the courts in pursuit of state habeas corpus relief. We think this holding is inconsistent with our decision two Terms ago in *Pennsylvania v. Finley*. . . . and rests on a misreading of our decision in *Bounds v. Smith* [1977]. . . .

In *Finley* we ruled that neither the Due Process Clause of the Fourteenth Amendment nor the equal protection guarantee of "meaningful access" required the State to appoint counsel for indigent prisoners seeking state postconviction relief. . . . [W]e held in *Ross v. Moffitt*, . . . that the right to counsel [for trial and for initial appeals] . . . did not carry over to a discretionary appeal provided by [state] law from the intermediate appellate court to the [state] [s]upreme [c]ourt. . . . We contrasted the trial stage of a criminal proceeding, where the State by presenting witnesses and arguing to a jury attempts to strip from the defendant the presumption of innocence and convict him of a crime, with the appellate stage of such a proceeding, where the defendant needs an attorney "not as a shield to protect him against being 'hauled into court' by the State and stripped of his presumption of innocence, but rather as a sword to upset the prior determination of guilt."

We held in *Finley* that the logic of *Ross v. Moffitt* required the conclusion that there was no federal constitutional right to counsel for indigent prisoners seeking state postconviction relief. . . .

Respondents, like the courts below, believe that *Finley* does not dispose of respondents' constitutional claim to appointed counsel in habeas proceedings because *Finley* did not involve the death penalty. . . .

We think that these cases require the conclusion that the rule of *Pennsylvania v. Finley* should apply no differently in capital cases than in noncapital cases. State collateral proceedings are not constitutionally required as an adjunct to the state criminal proceedings and serve a different and more limited purpose than either trial or appeal. The additional safeguards imposed by the Eighth Amendment at the trial stage of a capital case [i.e., requirements about jury procedures and consideration of aggravating and mitigating factors] are, we think, sufficient to assure the reliability of the process by which the death penalty is imposed. We therefore decline to read either the Eighth Amendment or the Due Process Clause to require yet another distinction between the rights of capital case defendants and those in noncapital cases.

The dissent opines that the rule that it would constitutionally mandate "would result in a net benefit to Virginia." . . . But this "mother knows best" approach should play no part in traditional constitutional adjudication. Even as a matter of policy, the correctness of the dissent's view is by no means self-evident. If, as we said in *Barefoot v. Estelle*, . . . direct appeal is the primary avenue for review of capital cases as well as other sentences, Virginia may quite sensibly decide to concentrate the resources it devotes to providing attorneys for capital defendants at the trial and appellate stages of a capital proceeding. Capable lawyering there would mean fewer colorable claims of ineffective assistance of counsel to be litigated on collateral attack. . . .

Justice O'CONNOR concurring:

I join in THE CHIEF JUSTICE's opinion. As his opinion demonstrates, there is nothing in the Constitution or the precedents of this Court which requires that a State provide counsel in postconviction proceedings. A postconviction proceeding is not part of the criminal process itself, but is instead a civil action designed to overturn a presumptively valid criminal judgment. Nothing in the Constitution requires the States to provide such proceedings, . . . nor does it seem to me that the Constitution requires the States to follow any particular federal model in those

proceedings. . . . [T]he matter is one of legislative choice based on difficult policy considerations and the allocation of scarce legal resources.
Our decision today rightly leaves these issues to resolution by Congress
and the state legislatures.

Justice KENNEDY concurring in judgment [joined by Justice O'CON-
NOR]:

It cannot be denied that collateral relief proceedings are a central part of
the review process for prisoners sentenced to death. As Justice
STEVENS observes, a substantial proportion of these prisoners succeed
in having their death sentences vacated in habeas corpus proceedings. . . .
The complexity of our jurisprudence in this area, moreover, makes it unlikely that capital defendants will be able to file successful petitions for
collateral relief without the assistance of persons learned in law. . . .

Unlike Congress, this Court lacks the capacity to undertake the
searching and comprehensive review called for in this area, for we can
decide only the case before us. While Virginia has not adopted procedures for securing representation that are as far reaching and effective as
those available in other States, no prisoner on death row in Virginia has
been unable to obtain counsel to represent him in postconviction proceedings, and Virginia's prison system is staffed with institutional lawyers
to assist in preparing petitions for postconviction relief. I am not prepared to say that this scheme violates the Constitution.

Justice STEVENS dissenting [joined by Justices BRENNAN, MAR-
SHALL, and BLACKMUN]:

Two Terms ago this Court reaffirmed that the Fourteenth Amendment
to the Federal Constitution obligates a State "to assure the indigent defendant an adequate opportunity to present his claims fairly in the context of the State's appellate process." . . . The narrow question presented
is whether that obligation includes appointment of counsel of indigent
death row inmates who wish to pursue state postconviction relief. View-
ing the facts in light of our precedents, we should answer that question in
the affirmative. . . .

II

These precedents demonstrate that the appropriate question in this case
is not whether there is an absolute "right to counsel" in collateral pro-

ceedings, but whether due process requires that these respondents be appointed counsel in order to pursue legal remedies. Three critical differences between *Finley* and this case demonstrate that even if it is permissible to leave an ordinary prisoner to his own resources in collateral proceedings, it is fundamentally unfair to require an indigent death row inmate to initiate collateral review without counsel's guiding hand. I shall address each of these differences in turn.

First. These respondents, like petitioners in *Powell* [*v. Alabama,* 1932], have been condemned to die. Legislatures conferred greater access to counsel on capital defendants than on persons facing lesser punishment even in colonial times. . . .

The unique nature of the death penalty not only necessitates additional protections during pretrial, guilt, and sentencing phases, but also enhances the importance of the appellate process. . . .

. . . There is . . . significant evidence that in capital cases what is ordinarily considered direct review does not sufficiently safeguard against miscarriages of justice to warrant this presumption of finality [for initial appeals prior to postconviction actions]. [After completion of initial appeals] [f]ederal habeas corpus courts granted initial relief in 0.25% to 7% of noncapital cases in recent years; in striking contrast the success rate in capital cases ranged from 60% to 70%. Such a high incidence of uncorrected error demonstrates that the meaningful appellate review necessary in a capital case extends beyond the direct appellate process.

Second. In contrast to the collateral process discussed in *Finley,* Virginia law contemplates that some claims ordinarily heard on direct review will be relegated to postconviction proceedings. Claims that trial or appellate counsel provided constitutionally ineffective assistance, for instance, usually cannot be raised until this [later] stage. . . . Given the irreversibility of capital punishment, such information deserves searching, adversarial scrutiny even if it is discovered after the close of direct review. . . .

Third. As the District court's findings reflect, the plight of the death row inmate constrains his ability to wage collateral attacks far more than does the lot of the ordinary inmate considered in *Finley.* The District Court found that the death row inmate has an extremely limited period to prepare and present his postconviction petition and any necessary applications for stays of execution. . . . Unlike the ordinary inmate, who presumably has ample time to use and reuse the prison library and to seek guidance from other prisoners experienced in preparing *pro se* petitions, . . . a grim deadline imposes a finite limit on the condemned person's capacity for useful research. . . .

III

Although in some circumstances governmental interests may justify infringements on Fourteenth Amendment rights, . . . Virginia has failed to assert any interest that outweighs respondents' right to legal assistance. The State already appoints counsel to death row inmates who succeed in filing postconviction petitions asserting at least one nonfrivolous claim; therefore, the additional cost of providing its 32 death row inmates competent counsel to prepare such petitions should be minimal. . . . Furthermore, multiple filings delay the conclusion of capital litigation and exacerbate the already serious burden these cases impose on the State's judicial system and the legal department. It seems obvious that professional preparation of the first postconviction petition, by reducing successive petitions, would result in a net benefit to Virginia. . . .

IV

The basic question in this case is whether Virginia's procedure for collateral review of capital convictions and sentences assures its indigent death row inmates an adequate opportunity to present their claims fairly. The District Court and Court of Appeals en banc found that it did not, and neither the State nor this Court's majority provides any reasoned basis for disagreeing with their conclusion. Simple fairness requires that this judgment be affirmed.

I respectfully dissent.

BUTLER v. McKELLAR

110 S. Ct. 1212 (1990)

Chief Justice REHNQUIST delivered the opinion of the Court [joined by Justices WHITE, O'CONNOR, SCALIA, and KENNEDY]:

Petitioner Horace Butler was convicted and sentenced to death for the murder of Pamela Lane. After his conviction became final on direct appeal, Butler collaterally attacked his conviction by way of a petition for federal habeas corpus. Butler relied on our decision in *Arizona v. Roberson* [1988], . . . decided after his conviction became final on direct appeal. We have held, however, that a new decision generally is not applicable in cases on collateral review unless the decision was dictated by precedent existing at the time the petitioner's conviction became final. . . .

Petitioner Butler was arrested six weeks [after the murder of Pamela

Lane] on an unrelated assault and battery charge. After invoking his Fifth Amendment right to counsel, Butler retained counsel who appeared with him at a bond hearing. . . . He was unable to make bond, however, and was returned to the county jail. Butler's attorney would later contend in state collateral relief proceedings that after the bond hearing, he had told the police officers not to question Butler further. The officers testified that they remembered no such instruction.

Early in the morning of September 1, 1980, Butler was taken from the jail to the Charleston County Police station. He was then informed for the first time that he was a suspect in Lane's murder. After receiving *Miranda* warnings, . . . Butler indicated that he understood his rights and signed two "waiver of rights" forms. The police then interrogated Butler about the murder. Butler did not request his attorney's presence at any time during the interrogation. . . .

The State indicted Butler and brought him to trial on a charge of first-degree murder. . . . The jury found [him] guilty and, in a separate proceeding, sentenced him to death concluding that he committed the murder during the commission of a rape. . . .

In May 1986, Butler filed this petition for federal habeas corpus relief. . . . [O]ne question raised in the petition was "whether police had the right to initiate questioning about the murder knowing petitioner had retained an attorney for the assault charge." . . .

On the same day the [Court of Appeals] denied Butler's rehearing petitions, we handed down our decision in *Roberson*. We held in *Roberson* that the Fifth Amendment bars police-initiated interrogation following a suspect's request for counsel in the context of a separate investigation. . . . The interrogation of Butler, while unquestionably contrary to present "guidelines" [after *Roberson*], was conducted in strict accordance with established law at the time. The [Court of Appeals] panel, therefore, denied Butler's petition for rehearing. . . .

Last Term in *Penry v. Lynaugh*, . . . we held that in both capital and noncapital cases, "new rules will not be applied or announced in cases on collateral review unless they fall into one of two exceptions." . . .

The "new rule" principle . . . validates reasonable, good-faith interpretations of existing precedents made by state courts even though they are shown to be contrary to later decisions. . . .

Butler contends that *Roberson* did not establish a new rule and is, therefore, available to support his habeas petition. Butler argues that *Roberson* was merely an application of *Edwards* [*v. Arizona*, 1981] to a slightly different set of facts. . . .

But the fact that a court says that its decision is within the "logical compass" of an earlier decision, or indeed that it is "controlled" by a prior decision, is not conclusive for purposes of deciding whether the current decision is a "new rule" under *Teague* [*v. Lane*, 1989]. . . . In *Roberson*, for instance, the Court found *Edwards* controlling but acknowledged a significant difference of opinion on the part of several lower courts that had considered the question previously. . . . [T]he outcome in *Roberson* was susceptible to debate among reasonable minds. . . . We hold, therefore, that *Roberson* announced a "new rule."

The question remains whether the new rule in *Roberson* nevertheless comes within one of the two recognized exceptions under which a new rule is available on collateral review. Under the first exception, "a new rule should be applied retroactively if it places 'certain kinds of primary, private individual conduct beyond the power of the criminal law-making authority to proscribe.' " . . . This exception is clearly inapplicable. . . .

Under the second exception, a new rule may be applied on collateral review "if it requires the observance of 'those procedures that . . . are "implicitly in the concept of ordered liberty." ' " . . . Because the violation of *Roberson's* added restrictions on police investigatory procedures would not seriously diminish the likelihood of obtaining an accurate determination—indeed, it may increase that likelihood—we conclude that *Roberson* did not establish any principle that would come within the second exception.

The judgment of the Court of Appeals [denying retroactive application of the *Roberson* principle to the improper interrogation of Butler] is therefore *Affirmed.*

Justice BRENNAN dissenting [joined by Justices MARSHALL, BLACK-MUN, and STEVENS]:

Last Term in *Teague v. Lane* [1989], . . . this Court manifested its growing hostility toward Congress' decision to authorize federal collateral review of state criminal convictions, curtailing the writ of habeas corpus by dramatically restructuring the retroactivity doctrine. The Court declared that a federal court entertaining a state prisoner's habeas petition generally may not reach the merits of the legal claim unless the court determines, as a threshold matter, that a favorable ruling on the claim would flow from the application of legal standards " 'prevailing at the time [the petitioner's] conviction became final.' " . . .

Today, under the guise of fine-tuning the definition of "new rule," the Court strips state prisoners of virtually *any* meaningful federal review of the constitutionality of their incarceration. . . . Put another way, a state prisoner can secure habeas relief only by showing that the state court's rejection of the constitutional challenge was *so* clearly invalid under then-prevailing legal standards that the decision could not be defended by any reasonable jurist. With this requirement, the Court has finally succeeded in its thinly veiled crusade to eviscerate Congress' habeas corpus regime.

I

. . . [T]he Court embraces a virtually all-encompassing definition of "new rule" without pausing to articulate any justification therefor. Result, not reason, propels the Court today. . . .

It is clear from our opinion in *Roberson* that we would have reached the identical conclusion had that case reached us in 1983 when Butler's conviction became final. In *Roberson*, we simply applied the legal principle established in *Miranda* and reconfirmed in *Edwards* to a set of facts that was not dissimilar in any salient way. We did not articulate any *new* principles of Fifth Amendment jurisprudence that were not already established in 1983.

Yet today the Court classifies *Roberson* as a "new rule" *notwithstanding* the above, characterizing the "outcome in *Roberson* [as] susceptible to debate among reasonable minds." . . . For this conclusion, the majority appears to rely solely on the fact that the court below and several state courts had incorrectly predicted the outcome in *Roberson* by holding that the *Edwards* rule ought not to apply where the second interrogation involves different subject matter. . . . But this reliance is perplexing. The majority might mean to suggest that a particular result is reasonable so long as a certain number of courts reach the same result. But this would be an odd criterion for "reasonableness." Its application would be ad hoc, both because there appears to be no principled basis for choosing any particular number of courts whose agreement is required before the result is deemed "reasonable," and because the criterion ultimately rests on a bootstrap to the extent that the later courts reaching the result simply rely on the earlier courts' having done the same. . . .

II

The Court's exceedingly broad definition of "new rule"—and conversely its narrow definition of "prevailing" law—betrays a vision of adjudication fundamentally at odds with any this Court has previously recognized. . . . The inability of lower courts to predict significant reformulations by this Court of the principles underlying prior precedents does not excuse them from the obligation to draw reasoned conclusions from principles that are well established at the time of their decisions. . . .

. . . [T]oday's decision, essentially foreclosing habeas review as an alternative "avenue of vindication," overrides Congress' will and leaves federal judicial protection of fundamental constitutional rights during the state criminal process solely to this Court upon direct review. I share Congress' lack of confidence in such a regime. After today, despite constitutional defects in the state processes leading to their conviction or sentencing, state prisoners will languish in jail—and others like Butler will die—because state courts were reasonable, even though wrong.

The majority apparently finds such injustice acceptable based upon an asserted " 'interest in leaving concluded litigation in a state of repose.' " . . . This will not do. It is one thing to preclude federal habeas petitioners from asserting claims based on legal principles contrary to or at least significantly dissimilar from those in existence at the time their convictions became final; such a basis for habeas relief engenders the possibility of " '*continually* forc[ing] the States to marshal resources in order to keep in prison defendants whose trial and appeals conformed to then-existing constitutional standards.' " . . . It is a *far* different thing to say that concerns for repose and resource scarcity justify today's judicial decision to protect States from the consequences of retrying or resentencing defendants whose trials and appeals *did not* conform to then-existing constitutional standards but are viewed as suffering from only "reasonable" defects. "This Court has never held . . . that finality, standing alone, provides a sufficient reason for federal courts to compromise their protection of constitutional rights under [habeas corpus actions]." . . .

III

It is Congress and not this Court who is " 'responsible for defining the scope of the writ [of habeas corpus].' " . . . Yet the majority, whose Members often pride themselves on their reluctance to play an "activist" judicial role by infringing upon legislative prerogatives, does not hesitate today to dismantle Congress' extension of federal habeas to state prisoners. Hereafter, federal habeas relief will be available in only the most egregious cases, in which state courts have flouted applicable Supreme Court precedent that cannot be distinguished on any arguable basis. I must dissent from this curtailment of the writ [of habeas corpus'] capacity for securing individual liberty. . . .

Questions

1. Without considering the later *Tison* case, what rule was created (or appeared to be created) in *Enmund* regarding the possibility of the death penalty for felony-murder accomplices who did not kill and did not intend to kill?
2. Justice O'Connor and her dissenting colleagues disagreed vigorously with the majority opinion in *Enmund*. Given O'Connor's strong belief that the *Enmund* decision was wrong (e.g., she accused the majority of acting "disin-

genuously"), was she inconsistent to support the *Enmund* decision in her *Tison* opinion? Why did O'Connor and her colleagues leave *Enmund* intact instead of following their true beliefs by reversing this precedent with which they so strongly disagreed?

3. Look closely at the composition of the majorities in *Enmund* and *Tison*. Which justice did O'Connor have to persuade and "capture" with her *Tison* opinion in order to gain a majority?

4. Who was the author of the *Enmund* majority opinion which created the apparently clear rule prohibiting the death penalty for felony-murder accomplices who lack "intent to kill"? If the *Tison* majority had sought to reverse *Enmund*, could they have attracted Justice White to their side? How would Justice White appear to legal commentators if he had agreed with a *Tison* opinion which reversed *Enmund*?

5. Did Justice O'Connor tailor her *Tison* opinion to appear to uphold the *Enmund* opinion, an opinion she originally rejected, simply to induce Justice White to join the *Tison* majority without forcing him to reject his own prior opinion?

6. Although *Tison* upholds *Enmund*, does the *Enmund* rule still actually exist? Is Justice Brennan correct in claiming that the *Tison* decision will increase discretionary, arbitrary death penalty decisions, and thus nullify the previously clear rule from *Enmund*?

7. In *Tison*, Justice Brennan accuses Justice O'Connor of selectively presenting facts in order to reach her conclusion that the Tisons' behavior fits her conception of "reckless disregard for human life." Is it significant that at the time of the highly publicized murders in *Tison*, O'Connor was a state judge in Arizona and presumably was quite familiar with the case from reading Arizona newspapers as the shocking events unfolded? Could personal familiarity with a case make a justice overzealous in his or her efforts to see someone severely punished for a horrible crime? [NOTE: Although O'Connor's characterization of the facts is subject to dispute, her conclusion supporting the death penalty for felony-murder accomplices is perfectly consistent with her conclusions in *Enmund*. After all, she was willing to have capital punishment applied to *Enmund* whose less horrible crime occurred in an unfamiliar state (Florida)].

8. Assume in *McCleskey* that the Georgia system is actually infused with racial discrimination, but there are not overt statements by prosecutors, judges, or juries indicating the existence of prejudice. According to the standards applied by the majority, is there any evidence that the Court would accept to prove the existence of systemic discrimination?

9. Why does the Court accept statistical evidence of discrimination in jury selection and employment discrimination cases but not in death penalty cases? Is Justice Powell's justification persuasive?

10. In *McCleskey*, why is the Court majority so reluctant to interfere with the discretionary decisions of actors within the criminal justice system?

11. Did the Court majority adequately consider and utilize the sophisticated social science evidence on racial discrimination? Even if Prof. Baldus addressed the specific methodological criticisms made by the lower courts,

could social science evidence ever adequately "prove" discrimination in capital sentencing to the satisfaction of the majority?

12. Did the majority in *McCleskey* adequately focus on "fairness" issues? Did the Court place excessive emphasis on the four policy considerations that Justice Brennan claimed were being weighed against the racial discrimination claim?

13. Was Justice Stevens' *McCleskey* dissent correct in observing that "[t]he Court's decision appears to be based on a fear that acceptance of McCleskey's claim would sound the death knell for capital punishment in Georgia"? If true, is this an appropriate factor for the Court to consider in its decision in the case?

14. Does Chief Justice Rehnquist's plurality opinion in *Murray* give adequate attention to "fairness" issues? Does Justice Kennedy agree with Rehnquist about the importance or "central[ity]" of postconviction petitions in capital cases? If not, why does Kennedy concur in the judgment?

15. In *Murray*, is Justice Stevens persuasive in arguing that death row inmates need and deserve more legal resources for postconviction petitions than do other prisoners?

16. How significant is Justice Stevens' claim that 60% to 70% of death penalty convictions are found to be defective by federal judges *after* they have already had complete review and endorsement by state appellate courts? Are there differences in the tenure and selection processes between state and federal judges which might affect their respective abilities to evaluate and overturn murder convictions? Why is the high percentage of successful postconviction petitions not discussed by Chief Justice Rehnquist's plurality opinion?

17. In *Butler*, all of the justices concluded that, under the *Roberson* rule, Butler's rights were violated when he was questioned by the police about the murder case outside of the presence of his attorney for the assault case. Why then does the majority refuse to permit Butler to have the issue recognized by the federal courts through the habeas corpus process?

18. Does the Court majority give adequate consideration to "fairness" issues in *Butler*? If a case identical to Butler's arose a few years (or even a few months) later, that defendant would have received a new trial because of the *Roberson* decision. By contrast, Butler is scheduled to be executed despite the use of improper police procedures to obtain a confession from him. Does this affect your assessment of the "fairness" issue?

19. If Congress created the opportunity for postconviction petitions through the habeas corpus statute, should the Supreme Court limit prisoners' access to the courts through the *Butler* retroactivity doctrine?

20. What values and policy considerations are emphasized by the majority (and plurality) in *McCleskey, Murray,* and *Butler*? What values and policy considerations are emphasized by the dissenters? Are either side's preferred outcomes "clearly correct" according to the words of the Constitution?

21. The vote of a single justice can frequently have a profound impact upon the

development of constitutional law and public policy. How would capital punishment policy be different if the dissenters in these three cases had been able to persuade a single, additional colleague to join them? How would other political actors and institutions have reacted if these three cases had been decided in accordance with the views of the dissenters?

SEVEN

The Supreme Court
and Political Opposition

The justices of the Supreme Court are the authoritative interpreters of the Constitution. Despite their authority to decide controversial issues, the justices' decisions do not necessarily finalize and put to rest the issues brought before them. In a formal sense, the power of "judicial review," which permits the Supreme Court to judge the constitutionality of acts by Congress, the President, and the states, appears to place the judiciary above the other governmental branches. In reality, however, other political actors can react to judicial decisions and thereby reshape and perpetuate the controversies that have been the subjects of court cases. Thus, if other political institutions are actively interested in an issue, they can draw the Supreme Court into an interactive process in which the Court will face the same issues repeatedly, albeit in slightly modified forms.

The abortion controversy provides an illustration of the Supreme Court's role in interacting with other institutions within the political system. In 1973, when the Supreme Court decided *Roe v. Wade*, a strong, seven-member majority articulated a definite, clear constitutional right for women to make choices concerning their own abortions during the first six months of pregnancy. The Court severely restricted the ability of states to regulate abortions or otherwise interfere with women's right of choice.

If Supreme Court decisions were guided by consistent legal principles or if the Court were truly the "final arbiter" of controversial issues, then *Roe v. Wade* should have firmly established a secure right to abortion protected by the Constitution. Constitutional law is, however, the product of politics. Supreme Court decisions are determined by justices' attitudes, values, and policy preferences. Moreover, other political insti-

129

tutions influence case outcomes through their interactions with the Supreme Court. The political interactions spurred by the Court's controversial opinion in Roe ultimately led to changes in the Court's decisions concerning abortion. Thus, constitutional law and public policy are fluid and change in response to the political and social environment.

The Supreme Court's decision in Roe did not settle the abortion issue. Anti-abortion political interest groups mobilized and attempted to influence voters, individual politicians, and legislatures. City councils, state legislatures, and Congress reacted to Roe v. Wade by enacting new legislation to regulate abortions. These laws sought to test the limits of the Supreme Court's decision and thereby push the Court toward approving greater governmental restrictions on abortion.

Instead of resolving the abortion issue, the decision in Roe v. Wade unleashed a flood of new cases upon the Supreme Court, each one requiring the Court to reconsider the abortion issue through examination of statutes passed in reaction to Roe. Over a fifteen-year period, the Court clarified and reaffirmed its decision in Roe by rejecting several state statutes (e.g., Thornburgh v. American College of Obstetricians and Gynecologists, 1986) and local ordinances (e.g., City of Akron v. Akron Center for Reproductive Health, 1984) that created restrictions on women's right of choice. However, the Court also approved a few statutes that interfered with the right of choice when a majority of justices found that those statutes did not clash with Roe. For example, the Court found that states and the federal government could refuse to pay for the abortions of poor women who relied upon public funding for their medical care (Maher v. Roe, 1977; Harris v. McRae, 1980). Thus, anti-abortion interests enjoyed some success in their efforts to write new laws that would limit opportunities for abortions.

During the 1980s, President Reagan reacted to the Supreme Court's support for abortion by seeking to appoint new justices who would oppose the abortion policy established in Roe v. Wade. In 1989, President Reagan had sufficiently altered the composition of the Court, by appointing three new justices and elevating a fourth to Chief Justice, that a new majority formed on the issue of abortion. In Webster v. Reproductive Health Services (1989), the new majority approved a Missouri statute which contained elements (e.g., a statutory declaration that life begins at conception) that had been rejected in previous cases. Over the course of sixteen years, reactions by various actors in a changing political environment led to an alteration in constitutional law and public policy affecting abortion. The Supreme Court is an important and influential actor in the continuing controversy over abortion. Despite its formal power to define constitutional law, however, it is but one actor within the political interactions that eventually determine law and public policy.

The cases reprinted in this chapter illustrate the Supreme Court's role in the political interactions affecting another controversial issue: burning the American flag as a form of symbolic speech. In contrast to the abortion cases, the opposing coalitions within the deeply divided Court on the flag burning issue have not formed along ideological lines. In *Texas v. Johnson* (1989), Justices Scalia and Kennedy, who are generally regarded as politically "conservative," joined three "liberal" justices (Brennan, Marshall, and Blackmun) to invalidate a state statute which made it a crime to burn an American flag. Because of the public outcry over this unpopular decision, politicians did not accept the Supreme Court's decision as the final word on this constitutional issue. The reactions of political actors were embodied in a *New York Times* headline describing the President's posture on the issue: "Bush Seeking Way to Circumvent Court's Decision on Flag Burning."[1] President Bush reacted to the decision by suggesting that the Constitution be amended to prevent flag burning. In effect, because he objected to the Court's decision, Bush sought to use the political process for amending the Constitution as a means of removing the flag burning issue from the Supreme Court's jurisdiction.

Congress ultimately passed a statute against flag burning. When the statute went into effect, protesters immediately burned flags in order to test the new law. It normally takes several years for an issue to work its way through the court system to reach the Supreme Court. For example, in *Texas v. Johnson*, the protester burned a flag at the 1984 Republican Convention but his case was not decided by the Supreme Court until 1989. The Supreme Court expedited its consideration of the new federal statute and reconsidered the flag-burning issue less than one year after the federal act's passage. The continuing political controversy over flag burning apparently led the Court to accelerate its consideration of the issue.

According to the *New York Times*, although "there was no mention [during oral arguments] of the political turbulence set off by the issue," many observers predicted that Justice Harry Blackmun might change sides and support the constitutionality of the statute.[2] When the five justices, including Justice Blackmun, ultimately maintained their position in *United States v. Eichman* (1990), by striking down the federal statute, members of Congress reacted by proposing a constitutional amendment

---

1. Bernard Weinraub, "Bush Seeking Way to Circumvent Court's Decision on Flag Burning," *New York Times*, June 27, 1989, at 1.

2. Neil A. Lewis, "Supreme Court Roundup: Arguments on Flag Burning Heard," *New York Times*, May 15, 1990, p. A6.

to protect the flag. The proposed amendment said: "Congress and the states shall have power to prohibit the physical desecration of the flag of the United States." After vigorous debate, majorities in the Senate and House of Representatives voted for the amendment, but the amendment failed because supporters lacked the required two-thirds majorities in both houses.[3] Many Republican politicians believed that the Supreme Court had given them an issue which they could utilize for partisan purposes in the 1990 Congressional elections.

The reactions and strategies of political actors opposed to the Court's decisions on this continuing controversy illuminate the Supreme Court's role in the interactive political process that defines and changes constitutional law and public policy.

UNITED STATES v. O'BRIEN

391 U.S. 367 (1968)

Chief Justice WARREN delivered the opinion of the Court [joined by Justices BLACK, FORTAS, BRENNAN, WHITE, STEWART, and HARLAN. Justice MARSHALL did not participate in the case]:

On the morning of March 31, 1966, David Paul O'Brien and three companions burned their Selective Service registration certificates on the steps of the South Boston Courthouse. A sizable crowd, including several agents of the Federal Bureau of Investigation, witnessed the event. Immediately after the burning, members of the crowd began attacking O'Brien and his companions. An FBI agent ushered O'Brien to safety inside the courthouse. After he was advised of his right to counsel and to silence, O'Brien stated to FBI agents that he had burned his registration certificate because of his beliefs, knowing that he was violating federal law. He produced the charred remains of the certificate, which, with his consent, were photographed.

For this act, O'Brien was indicted, tried, convicted, and sentenced. ... He stated in argument to the jury that he burned the certificate publicly to influence others to adopt his antiwar beliefs, as he put it, "so that other people would reevaluate their positions with Selective Service,

---

3. In the House, the amendment fell thirty-four votes short of the necessary two-thirds majority required for approval. Steven A. Holmes, "Amendment to Bar Flag Desecration Fails in the House," *New York Times,* June 22, 1990, p. A1. In the Senate, the amendment was nine votes short of approval. "Senate Also Turns Down Flag-Burning Amendment," *Akron Beacon Journal,* June 27, 1990, p. A6.

with the armed forces, and reevaluate their place in the culture of today, to hopefully consider my position." . . .

. . . In District Court, O'Brien argued that the [statute] prohibiting the knowing destruction or mutilation of certificates was unconstitutional because it was enacted to abridge free speech and because it served no legitimate legislative purpose. . . .

I

. . . .

The classification certificate shows the registrant's name, Selective Service number, signature, and eligibility classification. It specifies whether he was so classified by his local board, an appeal board, or the President. It contains the address of his local board and the date the certificate was mailed. . . .

II

O'Brien first argues that the [statute] is unconstitutional as applied to him because his act of burning his registration certificate was protected "symbolic speech" within the First Amendment. His argument is that the freedom of expression which the First Amendment guarantees includes all modes of "communication of ideas by conduct," and that his conduct is within this definition because he did it in "demonstration against the war and against the draft."

We cannot accept the view that an apparently limitless variety of conduct can be labeled "speech" whenever the person engaging in the conduct intends thereby to express an idea. However, even on the assumption that the alleged communicative element in O'Brien's conduct is sufficient to bring into play the First Amendment, it does not necessarily follow that the destruction of a registration certificate is constitutionally protected activity. This Court has held that when "speech" and "nonspeech" elements are combined in the same course of conduct, a sufficiently important governmental interest in regulating the nonspeech conduct can justify incidental limitations on First Amendment freedoms. To characterize the quality of the governmental interest which must appear, the Court has employed a variety of descriptive terms: compelling; substantial; subordinating; paramount; cogent; strong. Whatever imprecision inheres in these terms, we think it clear that a government regulation is sufficiently justified if it is within the constitutional power of the Government; if it furthers an important or substantial governmental interest; if the governmental interest is unrelated to the suppression of free expression; and if the incidental restriction on alleged First Amendment freedoms is no greater than is essential to the furtherance of that interest. We find that the [statute at issue here] meets all of these requirements, and consequently that O'Brien can be constitutionally convicted for violating it.

The constitutional power of Congress to raise and support armies and to make all laws necessary and proper to that end is broad and sweeping. . . . The power of Congress to classify and conscript manpower for military service is "beyond question." . . . Pursuant to this power, Congress may establish a system of registration for individuals liable for training and service, and may require such individuals within reason to cooperate in the registration system. The issuance of certificates indicating the registration and eligibility classification of individuals is a legitimate and substantial administrative aid in the functioning of this system. And legislation to insure the continuing availability of issued certificates serves a legitimate and substantial purpose in the system's administration. . . .

Justice DOUGLAS dissenting:

The Court states that the constitutional power of Congress to raise and support armies is "broad and sweeping" and that Congress' power "to classify and conscript manpower for military services is 'beyond question.'" This is undoubtedly true in times when, by declaration of Congress, the nation is in a state of war. The underlying and basic problem in this case, however, is whether conscription is permissible in the absence of a declaration of war. That question has not been briefed nor was it presented in oral argument; but it is, I submit, a question upon which the litigants and the country are entitled to a ruling. . . .

STREET v. NEW YORK

394 U.S. 576 (1969)

Justice HARLAN delivered the opinion of the Court [joined by Justices STEWART, DOUGLAS, BRENNAN, and MARSHALL]:

Appellant Street has been convicted in the New York courts of violating [a statute] which makes it a misdemeanor "publicly [to] mutilate, deface, defile, or defy, trample upon, or cast contempt upon either by words or act [any flag of the United States]." . . . We must decide whether, in light of all the circumstances, that conviction denied to him rights of free expression protected by the First Amendment and assured against state infringement by the Fourteenth Amendment. . . .

According to evidence given at trial, the events which led to the conviction were these. Appellant testified that during the afternoon of June 6, 1966, he was listening to the radio in his Brooklyn apartment. He heard a news report that civil rights leader James Meredith had been shot by a sniper in Mississippi. Saying to himself, "They didn't protect him," appellant, himself a Negro, took from his drawer a neatly folded, 48-star American flag which he formerly displayed on national holidays. Appellant left his apartment and carried the still-folded flag to the nearby intersection of St. James Place and Lafayette Avenue. Appellant stood on the northeast corner of the intersection, lit the flag with a match, and dropped the flag on the pavement when it began to burn.

Soon thereafter, a police officer halted his patrol car and found the burning flag. The officer testified that he then crossed to the northwest corner of the intersection, where he found appellant "talking out loud" to a small group of persons. The officer estimated that there were some 30 persons on the corner near the flag and 5 to 10 on the corner with appellant. The officer testified that as he approached within 10 or 15 feet of appellant, he heard appellant say, "We don't need no damn flag," and that when he asked appellant whether he had burned the flag appellant replied: "Yes; that is my flag; I burned it. If they let that happen to Meredith we don't need an American flag." Appellant admitted making the latter response, but he denied that he said anything else and asserted he always had remained on the corner with the flag. . . .

Street argues that his conviction was unconstitutional for three different reasons. *First,* he claims that [the statute] is overbroad, both on its face and as applied because the section makes it a crime "publicly [to] defy . . . or cast contempt upon [an American flag] *by words.* . . ." (Emphasis added.) *Second,* he contends [the statute] is vague and imprecise because it does not clearly define the conduct which it forbids. *Third,* he asserts that New York may not constitutionally punish one who publicly destroys or damages an American flag as a means of protest, because such an act constitutes expression protected by the Fourteenth Amendment. We deem it unnecessary to consider the latter two arguments, for we hold that [the statute] was unconstitutionally applied in appellant's case because it permitted him to be punished merely for speaking defiant or contemptuous words about the American flag. In taking this course, we resist the pulls to decide the constitutional issues involved in this case on a broader basis than the record before us imperatively requires. . . .

II

. . . .

Moreover, even assuming that the record precludes the inference that appellant's conviction might have been based *solely* on his words, we are still bound to reverse if the conviction could have been based upon *both* his words and his act. . . .

III

. . . The sworn information which charged appellant with the crime of malicious mischief . . . recited not only that appellant had burned an American flag but also that he "[did] shout, 'If they did that to Meredith, we don't need an American Flag.' " . . . While it is true that at trial greater emphasis was placed upon appellant's action in burning the flag than upon his words, a police officer did testify to the utterance of the words. The State never announced that it was relying exclusively upon the burning. . . .

IV

In these circumstances, we can think of four governmental interests which might conceivably have been furthered by punishing appellant for his words: (1) an interest in deterring appellant from vocally inciting others to commit unlawful acts; (2) an interest in preventing appellant from uttering words so inflammatory that they would provoke others to retaliate physically against him, thereby causing a breach of the peace; (3) an interest in protecting the sensibilities of passers-by who might be shocked by appellant's words about the American flag; and (4) an interest in assuring that appellant, regardless of the impact of his words upon others, showed proper respect for our national emblem.

In the circumstances of his case, we do not believe that any of these interests may constitutionally justify appellant's conviction under [the statute] for speaking as he did. . . . [His words] amounted only to somewhat excited public advocacy of the idea that the United States should abandon, at least temporarily, one of its national symbols. It is clear that the Fourteenth Amendment prohibits the States from imposing criminal punishment for public advocacy of peaceful change in our institutions.

. . .

. . . Though it is conceivable that some listeners might have been moved to retaliate upon hearing appellant's disrespectful words, we cannot say that appellant's remarks were so inherently inflammatory as to come within that small class of "fighting words" which are "likely to provoke the average person to retaliation, and thereby cause a breach of the peace." *Chaplinsky v. New Hampshire* [1942]. . . .

We have no doubt that the constitutionally guaranteed "freedom to be intellectually . . . diverse or even contrary," and the "right to differ as to things that touch the heart of the existing order," encompass the freedom to express publicly one's opinions about our flag, including those opinions which are defiant or contemptuous.

Since appellant could not constitutionally be punished under [the statute] for his speech, and since we have found that he may have been so punished, his conviction cannot be permitted to stand. In so holding, we reiterate that we have no occasion to pass upon the validity of this conviction insofar as it was sustained by the state courts on the basis that Street could be punished for his burning of the flag, even though the burning was an act of protest. Nor do we perceive any basis for our Brother WHITE's fears that our decision may be taken to require reversal whenever a defendant is convicted for burning a flag in protest, following a trial at which his words have been introduced to prove some element of that offense. Assuming that such a conviction would otherwise pass constitutional muster, a matter about which we express no view, nothing in this opinion would render the conviction impermissible merely because an element of the crime was proved by the defendant's words rather than in some other way. . . .

We add that disrespect for our flag is to be deplored no less in these vexed times than in calmer periods of our history. . . . Nevertheless, we are unable to sustain a conviction that may have rested on a form of expression, however, distasteful, which the Constitution tolerates and protects. . . .

Chief Justice WARREN dissenting:

I dissent from the reversal of this judgment . . . because [the Court] has declined to meet and resolve the basic question presented in the case. . . .

. . . [T]he Court specifically refuses to decide [the flag burning] issue. Instead, it searches microscopically for the opportunity to decide the case on the peripheral . . . ground, holding that it is impossible to determine the basis for appellant's conviction. In my opinion a reading of the short trial record leaves no doubt that appellant was convicted solely for burning the American flag. . . .

III

I am in complete agreement with the general rule that this Court should not treat broad constitutional questions when narrow ones will suffice to dispose of the litigation. However, where only the broad question is presented, it is our task and responsibility to confront that question squarely and resolve it. In a time when the American flag has increasingly become an integral part of public protests, the constitutionality of the flag-desecration statutes enacted by all of the States and Congress is a matter of the most widespread concern. Both those who seek constitutional shelter for acts of flag desecration perpetuated in the course of a political protest and those who must enforce the law are entitled to know the scope of constitutional protection. The Court's explicit reservation of the constitutionality of flag-burning prohibitions encourages others to test in the streets the power of our States and National Government to impose criminal sanctions upon those who would desecrate the flag.

I believe that the States and the Federal Government do have the power to protect the flag from acts of desecration and disgrace. But because the court has not met the issue, it would serve no purpose to delineate my reasons for his view. . . .

Justice BLACK dissenting:

. . . .

It passes my belief that anything in the Federal Constitution bars a State from making the deliberate burning of the American flag an offense. It is immaterial to me that words are spoken in connection with the *burning*. It is the *burning* of the flag that the State has set its face against. . . . The talking that was done took place "as an integral part of conduct in violation of a valid criminal statute" against burning the American flag in public. I would therefore affirm this conviction.

Justice WHITE dissenting:

The Court has spun an intricate, technical web but I fear it has ensnared itself in its own remorseless logic and arrived at a result having no support in the facts of the case or the governing law. . . .

. . . I reach precisely the opposite conclusion; before Street's conviction can be either reversed or affirmed, the Court *must* reach and decide the validity of a conviction for flag burning. . . .

. . . True, the complaint referred to both burning and speaking and the statute permits conviction for either insulting words or physical desecration. But surely the Court has its tongue in its cheek when it infers from this record the possibility that Street was not convicted for burning the flag but only for the words he uttered. It is a distortion of the record to read it in this manner, as THE CHIEF JUSTICE convincingly demonstrates. . . .

Justice FORTAS dissenting:

I agree with the dissenting opinion filed by THE CHIEF JUSTICE, but I believe that it is necessary briefly to set forth the reasons why the States and the Federal Government have the power to protect the flag from acts of desecration committed in public. . . .

If a state statute provided that it is a misdemeanor to burn one's shirt or trousers or shoes on the public thoroughfare, it could hardly be asserted that the citizen's constitutional right is violated. . . . [I]t is hardly possible that [the protester's] claim to First Amendment shelter would prevail against the State's claim of right to avert danger to the public and to avoid obstruction to traffic as a result of the fire. . . .

. . . If, as I submit, it is permissible to prohibit the burning of personal property on a public sidewalk, there is no basis for applying a different rule to flag burning. And the fact that the law is violated for purposes of protest does not immunize the violator. . . .

One may not justify burning a house, even if it is his own, on the ground, however sincere, that he does so as a protest. One may not justify breaking the windows of a government building on that basis. Protest does not exonerate lawlessness. And the prohibition against flag burning on the public thoroughfare being valid, the misdemeanor is not excused merely because it is an act of flamboyant protest.

TEXAS v. JOHNSON

109 S. Ct. 2533 (1989)

Justice BRENNAN delivered the opinion of the Court [joined by Justices MARSHALL, BLACKMUN, SCALIA, and KENNEDY]:

After publicly burning an American flag as a means of political protest, Gregory Lee Johnson was convicted of desecrating a flag in violation of Texas law. This case presents the question whether the conviction is consistent with the First Amendment. We hold that it is not.

I

While the Republican National Convention was taking place in Dallas in 1984, respondent Johnson participated in a political demonstration dubbed the "Republican War Chest Tour." As explained in literature distributed by the demonstrators and in speeches made by them, the purpose of this event was to protest the policies of the Reagan administration and of certain Dallas-based corporations. The demonstrators marched through the Dallas streets, chanting political slogans and stopping at several corporate locations to stage "die-ins" intended to dramatize the consequences of nuclear war. On several occasions they spray-painted the walls of buildings and overturned potted plants, but Johnson himself took no part in such activities. He did, however, accept an American flag handed to him by a fellow protestor who had taken it from a flag pole outside one of the targeted buildings.

The demonstration ended in front of Dallas City Hall, where Johnson unfurled the American flag, doused it with kerosene, and set it on fire. While the flag burned, the protestors chanted, "America, the red, white, and blue, we spit on you." After the demonstrators dispersed, a witness to the flag-burning collected the flag's remains and buried them in his backyard. No one was physically injured or threatened with injury, though several witnesses testified that they had been seriously offended by the flag-burning.

Of the approximately 100 demonstrators, Johnson alone was charged with a crime. The only criminal offense with which he was charged was desecration of a venerated object. . . . After a trial, he was convicted, sentenced to one year in prison, and fined $2,000. . . .

II

Johnson was convicted of flag desecration for burning the flag rather than for uttering insulting words. . . .

The First Amendment literally forbids the abridgement only of "speech," but we have long recognized that its protection does not end at the spoken or written word. . . .

In deciding whether particular conduct possesses sufficient communicative elements to bring the First Amendment into play, we have asked whether "[a]n intent to convey a particularized message was present, and [whether] the likelihood was great that the message would be understood by those who viewed it." . . .

The State of Texas conceded for purposes of its oral argument in this case that Johnson's conduct was expressive conduct, . . . and this concession seems to us . . . prudent. . . . Johnson burned an American flag as part—indeed, as the culmination—of a political demonstration that coincided with the convening of the Republican Party and its renomination of Ronald Reagan for President. The expressive, overtly political nature of this conduct was both intentional and overwhelmingly apparent. . . . In these circumstances, Johnson's burning of the flag was conduct "sufficiently imbued with elements of communication," . . . to implicate the First Amendment.

III

. . . .

. . . [We] must decide whether Texas has asserted an interest in support of Johnson's conviction that is unrelated to the suppression of expression. . . . The State offers two separate interests to justify this conviction: preventing breaches of the peace, and preserving the flag as a symbol of nationhood and national unity. We hold that the first interest is not implicated on this record and that the second is related to the suppression of expression. . . .

. . . [N]o disturbance of the peace actually occurred or threatened to occur because of Johnson's burning of the flag. Although the State stresses the disruptive behavior of the protestors during their march toward City Hall, . . . it admits that "no actual breach of the peace occurred at the time of the flagburning or in response to the flagburning." . . .

Nor does Johnson's expressive conduct fall within that small class of "fighting words" that are "likely to provoke the average person to retaliation, and thereby cause a breach of the peace." *Chaplinsky v. New Hampshire* [1942]. . . . No reasonable onlooker would have regarded Johnson's generalized expression of dissatisfaction with the policies of the Federal Government as a direct personal insult or an invitation to exchange fisticuffs. . . .

We thus conclude that the State's interest in maintaining order is not implicated on these facts. . . .

IV

. . . .

. . . According to Texas, if one physically treats the flag in a way that would tend to cast doubt on either the idea that nationhood or national unity are the flag's referents or that national unity actually exists, the message conveyed thereby is a harmful one and therefore may be prohibited.

If there is a bedrock principle underlying the First Amendment, it is that the Government may not prohibit the expression of an idea simply because society finds the idea itself offensive or disagreeable. . . .

We have not recognized an exception to this principle even where our flag has been involved. . . .

In short, nothing in our precedents suggests that a State may foster

its own view of the flag by prohibiting expressive conduct relating to it.
. . .

Texas' focus on the precise nature of Johnson's expression, moreover, misses the point of our prior decisions: their enduring lesson, that the Government may not prohibit expression simply because it disagrees with its message, is not dependent on the particular mode in which one chooses to express an idea. . . .

. . . [W]e do not doubt that the Government has a legitimate interest in making efforts to "preserv[e] the national flag as an unalloyed symbol of our country." . . . To say that the Government has an interest in encouraging proper treatment of the flag, however, is not to say that it may criminally punish a person for burning a flag as a means of political protest. . . .

We are tempted to say, in fact, that the flag's deservedly cherished place in our community will be strengthened, not weakened, by our holding today. Our decision is a reaffirmation of the principles of freedom and inclusiveness that the flag best reflects, and of the conviction that our toleration of criticism such as Johnson's is a sign and source of our strength. Indeed, one of the proudest images of our flag, the one immortalized in our national anthem, is of the bombardment it survived at Fort McHenry. It is the Nation's resilience, not its rigidity, that Texas sees reflected in the flag—and it is that resilience that we reassert today.

The way to preserve the flag's special role is not to punish those who feel differently about these matters. It is to persuade them that they are wrong. . . . And, precisely because it is our flag that is involved, one's response to the flag-burner may exploit the uniquely persuasive power of the flag itself. We can imagine no more appropriate response to burning a flag than waving one's own, no better way to counter a flag-burner's message than by saluting the flag that burns, no surer means of preserving the dignity even of the flag that burned than by—as one witness here did—according its remains a respectful burial. We do not consecrate the flag by punishing its desecration, for in doing so we dilute the freedom that this cherished emblem represents.

V

Johnson was convicted for engaging in expressive conduct. The State's interest in preventing breaches of the peace does not support his conviction because Johnson's conduct did not threaten to disturb the peace. Nor does the State's interest in preserving the flag as a symbol of nationhood and national unity justify his criminal conviction for engaging in political expression. . . .

Justice KENNEDY concurring:

. . . .

The hard fact is that sometimes we must make decisions we do not like. We make them because they are right, right in the sense that the law and the Constitution, as we see them, compel the result. And so great is our commitment to the process that, except in the rare case, we do not pause to express distaste for the result, perhaps for fear of undermining a valued principle that dictates the decision. This is one of those rare cases. . . .

Chief Justice REHNQUIST dissenting [joined by Justices WHITE and O'CONNOR]:

. . . For more than 200 years, the American flag has occupied a unique position as the symbol of our Nation, a uniqueness that justifies a governmental prohibition against flag burning in the way respondent Johnson did here. . . .

The American flag, . . . throughout more than 200 years of our history, has come to be the visible symbol embodying our Nation. It does not represent the views of any particular political party, and it does not represent any particular political philosophy. The flag is not simply another "idea" or "point of view" competing for recognition in the marketplace of ideas. Millions and millions of Americans regard it with an almost mystical reverence, regardless of what sort of social, political, or philosophical beliefs they may have. I cannot agree that the First Amendment invalidates the Act of Congress and the laws of 48 of 50 States, which make criminal the public burning of the flag. . . .

Here it may equally well be said that the public burning of the American flag by Johnson was no essential part of any exposition of ideas, and at the same time it had a tendency to incite a breach of the peace. Johnson was free to make any verbal denunciation of the flag that he wished; indeed, he was free to burn the flag in private. He could publicly burn other symbols of the Government or effigies of political leaders. . . .

The Court concludes its opinion with a regrettably patronizing civics lecture, presumably addressed to the Members of both Houses of Congress, the members of the 48 state legislatures that enacted prohibitions against flag burning, and the troops fighting under that flag in Vietnam who objected to its being burned. . . . The Court's role as the final expositor of the Constitution is well established but its role as a platonic guardian admonishing those responsible to public opinion as if they were truant school children has no similar place in our system of government. . . .

... Uncritical extension of constitutional protection to the burning of the flag risks the frustration of the very purpose for which organized governments are instituted. The Court decides that the American flag is just another symbol, about which not only must opinions pro and con be tolerated, but for which the most minimal public respect may not be enjoined. The government may conscript men into the Armed Forces where they must fight and perhaps die for the flag, but the government may not prohibit the public burning of the banner under which they fight. I would uphold the Texas statute as applied in this case.

Justice STEVENS dissenting:

. . . .

A country's flag is a symbol of more than "nationhood and national unity." ... It also signifies the ideas that characterize the society that has chosen that emblem as well as the special history that has animated the growth and power of those ideas....

... I am unpersuaded [by the majority's arguments]. The creation of a federal right to post bulletin boards and graffiti on the Washington Monument might enlarge the market for free expression, but at a cost I would not pay. Similarly, in my considered judgment, sanctioning the public desecration of the flag will tarnish its value—both for those who cherish the ideas for which it waves and for those who desire to don the robes of martyrdom by burning it. That tarnish is not justified by the trivial burden on free expression occasioned by requiring that an available, alternative mode of expression—including uttering words critical of the flag . . .—be employed....

... Respondent was prosecuted because of the method he chose to express his dissatisfaction with [government] policies. Had he chosen to spray paint—or perhaps convey with a motion picture projector—his message of dissatisfaction on the facade of the Lincoln Memorial, there would be no question about the power of Government to prohibit his means of expression. The prohibition would be supported by the legitimate interest in preserving the quality of an important national asset. Though the asset at stake in this case is intangible, given its unique value, the same interest supports a prohibition of the desecration of the American flag.

The ideas of liberty and equality have been an irresistible force in motivating leaders like Patrick Henry, Susan B. Anthony, and Abraham Lincoln, schoolteachers like Nathan Hale and Booker T. Washington, the Philippine Scouts who fought at Bataan, and soldiers who scaled the bluff at Omaha Beach. If those ideas are worth fighting for—and our history demonstrates that they are—it cannot be true that the flag that uniquely symbolizes their power is not itself worthy of protection from unnecessary desecration.

I respectfully dissent.

FLAG PROTECTION ACT OF 1989

United States Code, Title 18, Section 700

Desecration of the flag of the United States; penalties

(a)(1) Whoever knowingly mutilates, defaces, physically defiles, burns, maintains on the floor or ground, or tramples upon any flag of the United States shall be fined under this title or imprisoned for not more than one year, or both.

(2) This subsection does not prohibit conduct consisting of the disposal of a flag when it has become worn or soiled.

(b) As used in this section, the term "flag of the United States" means any flag of the United States, or any part thereof, made of any substance, of any size, in a form that is commonly displayed. . . .

LEGISLATIVE HISTORY—FLAG PROTECTION ACT OF 1989

Senate Report No. 101-152, *U.S. Code Congressional and Administrative News* (1989), pp. 610–635.

. . . .

The flag has stood as the unique and unalloyed symbol of the Nation for more than 200 years. In seeking to protect its physical integrity, Congress is simply ratifying the unique status conferred upon the flag by virtue of its historic function as the emblem of this Nation. Furthermore, in granting protection to the flag, [the statute] does not seek to protect the flag as the embodiment of any single idea; indeed, the flag is worthy of protection not because it represents any one idea, but because it represents many ideas. As the testimony of every witness demonstrated, the flag represents different things to different people.

Congress' power to protect the physical integrity of the flag has never been questioned, and is consistent with its authority to protect symbols and landmarks. That power can properly be applied, moreover, even to those instances in which a person might seek to express an idea or convey a message through the destruction of the symbol or landmark. . . . The core principle is that in protecting those symbols or landmarks, the government cannot do so in a way that singles out or targets the message of whoever threatens it. . . .

[The statute] is consistent with the teachings of the Supreme Court in *Texas v. Johnson,* . . . that we can revere the flag and protect the flag as long as we do not do so in a manner that singles out or targets the message of whoever threatens it. . . . [This statute] amends the existing Federal flag statute . . . to make it content-neutral. . . .

There exists, then, strong and significant grounds—particularly based on Justice Blackmun's dissenting opinion in *Smith v. Goguen*[, a 1974 case concerning a flag sown onto the seat of a man's trousers in which Blackmun would have upheld a criminal conviction for violating a state flag protection statute,] and the accommodation of that view by the majority in *Texas v. Johnson*—to believe that the Court distinguishes between content-based statutes such as the Texas law struck down in *Johnson* and the existing Federal statute, and content-neutral statutes such as [this new federal statute], which do not single anyone out for prosecution based on the views he or she intended to express. . . .

MINORITY VIEWS OF SENATOR HOWARD METZENBAUM
[D-OHIO]

. . . .

Flag desecration is abhorrent. The American flag symbolizes the hard-won rights and liberties which make America great. Johnson's act was detestable, and it richly deserves the scorn of all Americans.

Nevertheless, the Court's decision in the *Johnson* case does not warrant a legislative response. . . .

The Court's decision in *Johnson* was a courageous and unpopular one. It illustrates the wisdom of allowing the Supreme Court to be the final arbiter of the Constitution, thereby preventing the sweep of its protection from varying according to the political passions of the day. The Bill of Rights is not designed to protect people or ideas that would win popularity contests. Indeed, the right to free expression is meaningless if that right only protects expression sanctioned by the majority. The depth of a nation's commitment to free speech is measured by its willingness to tolerate expression which most of its people find repellent.

The Court's decision in *Johnson* was grounded in these timeless and enduring principles. Rather than attempt to craft a legislative response to that decision, both the Constitution and the flag would be best served by having Congress do nothing. Legislation to protect the flag is not necessary. Respect for the flag is not under siege. American values and American security are not being threatened by an outbreak of flag desecration.

MINORITY VIEWS OF SENATORS ORRIN G. HATCH [R-UTAH] AND CHARLES E. GRASSLEY [R-IOWA]

. . . .

We have concluded that a constitutional amendment is absolutely necessary to ensure with certainty the validity of any statute banning flag desecration. . . .

S.J. 180 provides for the following amendment to the Constitution: "The Congress shall have power to prohibit the physical desecration of the Flag of the United States." We believe adoption of this amendment fulfills its intent to overturn the *Texas v. Johnson* decision and restore the power to Congress and the States to prohibit flag desecration which we believe they always had. . . .

UNITED STATES v. EICHMAN

110 S. Ct. 2404 (1990)

Justice BRENNAN delivered the opinion of the Court [joined by Justices MARSHALL, BLACKMUN, SCALIA, and KENNEDY]:

I

In these consolidated appeals, we consider whether appellees' prosecution for burning a United States flag in violation of the Flag Protection Act of 1989 is consistent with the First Amendment. Applying our recent decision in *Texas v. Johnson* (1989), the District Court held that the Act cannot constitutionally be applied to appellees. We affirm. . . .

II

Last term in *Johnson*, we held that a Texas statute criminalizing the desecration of venerated objects, including the United States flag, was unconstitutional as applied to an individual who had set such a flag on fire during a political demonstration. . . .

We reasoned that the state's asserted interest "in preserving the flag as a symbol of nationhood and national unity," was an interest "related 'to the suppression of free expression' within the meaning of *O'Brien*." . . . We therefore subjected the statute to 'the most exacting scrutiny.'" quoting *Boos v. Barry* (1988), and we concluded that the state's asserted interests could not justify the infringement on the demonstrator's First Amendment rights.

After our decision in *Johnson*, Congress passed the Flag Protection Act of 1989. . . .

The Government concedes in this case, as it must, that appellees' flag-burning constituted expressive conduct, but invites us to reconsider our rejection in *Johnson* of the claim that flag-burning as a mode of expression, like obscenity or "fighting words" does not enjoy the full protection of the First Amendment.... This we decline to do. The only remaining question is whether the Flag Protection Act is sufficiently distinct from the Texas statute that it may constitutionally be applied to proscribe appellees' expressive conduct.

The Government contends that the Flag Protection Act is constitutional because ... the Act does not target expressive conduct on the basis of the content of its message. The Government asserts an interest in "protect[ing] the physical integrity of the flag under all circumstances" in order to safeguard the flag's identity " 'as the unique and unalloyed symbol of the Nation.' "

The Act proscribes conduct (other than disposal) that damages or mistreats a flag, without regard to the actor's motive, his intended message, or the likely effects of his conduct on onlookers. By contrast, the Texas statute expressly prohibited only those acts of physical desecration "that the actor knows will seriously offend" onlookers, and the former Federal statute prohibited only those acts of desecration that "cas[t] contempt upon" the flag.

Although the Flag Protection Act contains no explicitly content-based limitation on the scope of prohibited conduct, it is nevertheless clear that the Government's asserted interest is "related 'to the suppression of free expression,' " and concerned with the content of such expression. . . .

But the mere destruction or disfigurement of a particular physical manifestation of the symbol, without more, does not diminish or otherwise affect the symbol itself in any way. For example, the destruction of a flag in one's own basement would not threaten the flag's recognized meaning. Rather, the Government's desire to preserve the flag as a symbol for certain national ideals is implicated "only when a person's treatment of the flag communicates [a] message" to others that is inconsistent with those ideals.

Moreover, the precise language of the Act's prohibitions confirms Congress's interest in the communicative impact of flag destruction. The Act criminalizes the conduct of anyone who "knowingly mutilates, defaces, physically defiles, burns, maintains on the floor or ground, or tramples upon any flag." Each of the specified terms—with the possible exception of "burns"—unmistakably connotes disrespectful treatment of the flag and suggests a focus on those acts likely to damage the flag's symbolic value. And the explicit exemption in Sec. 700 (a)(2) for disposal of "worn or soiled" flags protects certain acts traditionally associated with patriotic respect for the flag.

As we explained in *Johnson*: "[I]f we were to hold that a state may forbid flag-burning wherever it is likely to endanger the flag's symbolic role, but allow it wherever burning a flag promotes that role—as where, for example, a person ceremoniously burns a dirty flag—we would be . . . permitting a state to 'prescribe what shall be orthodox' by saying that one may burn the flag to convey one's attitude toward it and its referents only if one does not endanger the flag's representation of nationhood and national unity."

Although Congress cast the Flag Protection Act in somewhat broader terms than the Texas statute at issue in *Johnson*, the Act still suffers from the same fundamental flaw: it suppresses expression out of concern for its likely communicative impact. . . . [T]he Act therefore must be subjected to "the most exacting scrutiny," . . . and for the reasons stated in *Johnson*, the Government's interest cannot justify its infringement on First Amendment rights. We decline the Government's invitation to reassess this conclusion in light of Congress's recent recognition of a purported "national consensus" favoring a prohibition on flag-burning. Even assuming such a consensus exists, any suggestion that the Government's interest in suppressing speech becomes more weighty as popular opposition to that speech grows is foreign to the First Amendment.

III

. . . .

We are aware that desecration of the flag is deeply offensive to many. But the same might be said, for example, of virulent ethnic and religious epithets, . . . vulgar repudiations of the draft, . . . and scurrilous caricatures. . . . "If there is a bedrock principle underlying the First Amendment, it is that the Government may not prohibit the expression of an idea simply because society finds the idea itself offensive or disagreeable." . . . Punishing desecration of the flag dilutes the very freedom that makes this emblem so revered, and worth revering. . . .

Justice STEVENS dissenting [joined by Chief Justice REHNQUIST and Justices WHITE and O'CONNOR]:

The Court's opinion ends where proper analysis of the issue should begin. Of course "the Government may not prohibit the expression of an idea simply because society finds the idea itself offensive or disagreeable." None of us disagrees with that proposition. But it is equally well settled that certain methods of expression may be prohibited if (a) the prohibition is supported by a legitimate societal interest that is unrelated to suppression of the ideas the speaker desires to express; (b) the prohibition does not entail any interference with the speaker's freedom to express those ideas by other means; and (c) the interest in allowing the speaker complete freedom of choice among alternative methods of expression is less important than the societal interest supporting the prohibition.

Contrary to the position taken by counsel for the flag-burners in *Texas v. Johnson,* it is now conceded that the Federal Government has a legitimate interest in protecting the symbolic value of the American flag. Obviously that value cannot be measured, or even described, with any precision. It has at least these two components: in times of national crisis, it inspires and motivates the average citizen to make personal sacrifices in order to achieve societal goals of overriding importance; at all times, it serves as a reminder of the paramount importance of pursuing the ideals that characterize our society. . . .

The flag embodies the spirit of our national commitment to those ideals [of liberty, equality, and tolerance that Americans have passionately defended and debated throughout our history]. The message thereby transmitted does not take a stand upon our disagreements, except to say that those disagreements are best regarded as competing interpretations of shared ideals. It does not judge particular policies, except to say that they command respect when they are enlightened by the spirit of liberty and equality. To the world, the flag is our promise that we will continue to strive for these ideals. To us, the flag is a reminder both that the struggle for liberty and equality is unceasing, and that our obligation of tolerance and respect for all of our fellow citizens encompasses those who disagree with us—indeed, even whose ideas are disagreeable or offensive.

Thus, the Government may—indeed, it should—protect the symbolic value of the flag with regard to the specific content of the flag-burners' speech. The prosecution in this case does not depend upon the object of the defendants' protest. It is, moreover, equally clear that the prohibition does not entail any interference with the speaker's freedom to express his or her ideas by other means. It may well be true that other means of expression may be less effective in drawing attention to those ideas, but that is not itself a sufficient reason for immunizing flag burning. Presumably a gigantic fireworks display or a parade of nude models in a public park might draw even more attention to a controversial message, but such methods of expression are nevertheless subject to regulation.

The case therefore comes down to a question of judgment. Does the admittedly important interest in allowing every speaker to choose the method of expressing his or her ideas that he or she deems most effective and appropriate outweigh the societal interest in preserving the symbolic value of the flag? . . . The opinions in *Texas v. Johnson* demonstrate that reasonable judges may differ with respect to each of these judgments.

. . . The freedom of expression protected by the First Amendment embraces not only the freedom to communicate particular ideas, but also the right to communicate them effectively. That right, however, is not absolute—the communicative value of a well-placed bomb in the Capitol does not entitle it to the protection of the First Amendment.

Burning a flag is not, of course, equivalent to burning a public building. Assuming that the protester is burning his own flag and it causes no physical harm to other persons or their property. The impact is purely symbolic, and it is apparent that some thoughtful persons believe that impact, far from depreciating the value of the symbol, will actually enhance its meaning. I most respectfully disagree.

Indeed, what makes this case particularly difficult for me is what I regard as the damage to the symbol that has already occurred as a result of this Court's decision to place its stamp of approval on the act of flag-burning. A formerly dramatic expression of protest is now rather commonplace. In today's marketplace of ideas, the public burning of a Vietnam draft card is probably less provocative than lighting a cigarette. Tomorrow flag burning may produce a similar reaction. There is surely a direct relationship between the communicative value of the act of flag burning and the symbolic value of the object being burned.

The symbolic value of the American flag is not the same today that it was yesterday. Events during the last three decades have altered the country's image in the eyes of numerous Americans, and some now have difficulty understanding the message that the flag conveyed to their parents and grandparents—whether born abroad and naturalized or native born. Moreover, the integrity of the symbol has been compromised by those leaders who seem to advocate compulsory worship of the flag even by individuals whom it offends, or who seem to manipulate the symbol of national purpose into a pretext for partisan disputes about meaner ends. And, as I have suggested, the residual value of the symbol after this Court's decision in *Texas v. Johnson* is surely not the same as it was a year ago.

Given all these considerations, plus the fact that the Court today is really doing nothing more than reconfirming what it has already decided, it might be appropriate to defer to the judgment of the majority and merely apply the doctrine of *stare decisis* to the case at hand. That action, however, would not honestly reflect my considered judgment concerning the relative importance of the conflicting interests that are at stake. I

remain persuaded that the considerations identified in my opinion in
Texas v. Johnson are of controlling importance in this case as well.
Accordingly, I respectfully dissent.

Questions

1. In the Supreme Court's assessment of permissible regulation of expressive conduct, what is the difference between burning a draft card and burning a flag? Which object is more important? Why?
2. Why did the majority in *Street* sidestep the flag burning issue? Was it appropriate for them to do so?
3. In his dissent in *Street*, what compelling governmental interest does Justice Fortas identify that would permit a legislature to prohibit flag burning? Is this interest discussed in the subsequent flag burning cases?
4. What two governmental interests are asserted by Texas in the *Johnson* case? How does the majority analyze these interests?
5. Does flag burning strengthen or weaken "the flag's deservedly cherished place in our community"?
6. Do you agree with Chief Justice Rehnquist that the majority opinion in *Johnson* contains a "regrettably patronizing civics lecture" which treats elected officials "as if they were truant school children"?
7. Is Chief Justice Rehnquist correct in saying that men serving in American military forces "must fight and perhaps die for the flag"?
8. Is the American flag so special as a symbol that it deserves extra protection? What harm is caused if a flag is burned during a protest? What harm is caused if a flag is burned secretly in someone's basement? Are there any other special symbols that deserve special protection?
9. If alternative modes of expression are available, should the government be permitted to prosecute flag burners?
10. Does Justice Stevens present an appropriate analogy in comparing flag burning to painting slogans on the Lincoln Memorial? Should the legislative history of the Flag Protection Act equate "symbols" with "landmarks"? Does Justice Stevens' view change in *Eichman* when he says, "Burning a flag is not, of course, equivalent to burning a public building"?
11. Is the Flag Protection Act of 1989 "content neutral"?
12. Does the legislative history of the Flag Protection Act make an explicit attempt to induce Justice Blackmun to change sides by highlighting and praising Blackmun's 1974 dissent in *Smith v. Goguen*?
13. In *Eichman*, how does the majority analyze the purported governmental interests that would justify the Flag Protection Act?
14. Is a supposed national consensus against flag burning relevant to the judicial consideration of this issue? Should the interpretation of the Bill of Rights be sensitive to majoritarian consensus?
15. Compare the tone of the dissenting opinions in *Johnson* with the tone of Justice Stevens' dissent in *Eichman*. In *Eichman*, Stevens notes that "reasonable judges may differ with respect to . . . these judgments." Are the dis-

senters in *Eichman* trying to cool down the political firestorm that erupted
after *Johnson?*

16. Who is Stevens talking about when he says that "the integrity of the symbol
    has been compromised by those leaders who seem to advocate compulsory
    worship of the flag even by individuals whom it offends, or who seem to ma-
    nipulate the symbol of national purpose into a pretext for partisan disputes
    about meaner ends"? Is is surprising that Stevens, a Republican, is joined by
    two other Republicans (Rehnquist and O'Connor) in expressing this view?

17. Does the *Eichman* dissent signal that even those justices who would permit
    prosecution of flag burners do not think that the Constitution should be
    amended over this issue?

EIGHT

Interpersonal Relations and the Tone of Opinions

The Supreme Court's decisions are affected by the relationships and attitudes of the nine human beings who don black robes and assume responsibility for addressing society's most divisive issues. A justice's effectiveness within the Court is not merely the product of intelligent, forceful opinions but depends upon friendly, sensitive relationships with colleagues.

Justices must work together day after day, and because they can serve in office for life, they frequently work together for decades. The friction that may develop between individuals who work in such close quarters can fester and grow. As a result, interpersonal antagonisms can affect the Court's work. Although justices follow traditions designed to maintain cordial relationships, such as ritually shaking hands with all other justices each time they sit down to discuss cases, feuds have developed between justices in the past. During the 1920s and 1930s, for example, Justice James McReynolds demonstrated his personal abrasiveness and ethnic prejudice by leaving the room whenever Louis Brandeis, the first Jewish justice, spoke during the Court's weekly conferences.[1] In the early 1950s, Chief Justice Vinson once had to be physically restrained when he was upset by the remarks of another justice during conference.[2]

In order to form majorities to effectuate their legal theories and policy preferences, justices must persuade or induce colleagues to join their opinions. As the death penalty cases (*Enmund v. Florida* and *Tison v. Ar-*

---

1. David M. O'Brien, *Storm Center: The Supreme Court in American Politics*, 2nd ed. (New York: W. W. Norton, 1990), p. 281.
   2. Ibid.

izona) in Chapter 6 demonstrated, justices can manipulate the reasoning presented in their opinions to attract other justices to their perspectives. What if, however, there are personal animosities brewing between justices? Can these personal conflicts affect the formation of coalitions on particular cases? Because the justices are human beings whose opinions are influenced by their attitudes and feelings, interpersonal relations within the Court presumably can affect judicial decisions.

Although it is difficult to know how the justices relate to each other within the Court, the sharp comments that surface in justices' opinions raise questions about how these comments are received by other justices. The justices have, in general, maintained a tradition of politely and respectfully criticizing their colleagues' decisions with which they disagree. Some opinions, however, contain language which pointedly derides other justices. For example, Chief Justice Burger created a three-prong test for evaluating government actions that might improperly advance religion and thus implicate the Establishment Clause of the First Amendment (*Lemon v. Kurtzman*, 1971). The so-called "*Lemon* test" was consistently applied by the Court in subsequent Establishment Clause cases. In a 1984 challenge to the Nebraska legislature's policy of paying a Protestant chaplain to lead a prayer before each legislative session, Burger ignored the test he had created and approved Nebraska's practice. In dissent, Justice Brennan slammed the majority's inadequate analysis by implying that mere law students could have made a better decision: "I have no doubt that, if any group of law students were asked to apply the principles of *Lemon* to the question of legislative prayer, they would nearly unanimously find the practice to be unconstitutional." In dissenting from a decision approving an affirmative action program, Justice Rehnquist pointedly criticized the majority for inventing an unsupportable decision: "[B]y a tour de force reminiscent not of jurists such as Hale, Holmes, and Hughes, but of escape artists such as Houdini, the Court eludes clear statutory language" (*United Steelworkers of America v. Weber*, 1979). These and other examples indicate that, in crafting their opinions, justices sometimes choose to use language that does not merely express disagreement, but actually risks offending their colleagues.

In the late 1980s, as the composition of the Supreme Court changed through the inclusion of Reagan appointees and a new conservative majority began to emerge, commentators detected an increase in abrasive interchanges within the Court's opinions. Stuart Taylor characterizes the era as the "season of snarling justices."[3]

A key figure involved in the increasing number of opinions that lack

    3. Stuart Taylor, Jr., "Season of Snarling Justices," *Akron Beacon Journal*, April 5, 1990, p. A11.

the Court's traditional diplomatic, respectful tone is Justice Antonin Scalia. Although Scalia has only been a justice since 1986, his strident views and confrontational opinions show that he is a powerful voice within the Court. Scalia established his outspoken style while he was a law professor. For example, Justice Lewis Powell received praise for crafting a thoughtful compromise on the issue of affirmative action that forbade racial quotas but permitted limited programs to increase diversity (*Regents of the University of California v. Bakke*, 1978). Professor Scalia publicly condemned these legal developments by writing, "I frankly find this area [of law] an embarrassment to teach."[4] He labeled Justice Powell's decision "an historic trivialization of the Constitution."[5] When Justice Scalia subsequently arrived at the Supreme Court and, in fact, became Justice Powell's colleague, all eyes were on Justice Scalia to see whether he would modify his strident tone in order to cooperate with his colleagues. As the opinions reprinted in this chapter indicate, Scalia has not moderated his confrontational style.

The risks posed by Scalia's strident tone were most apparent in the controversial decision about abortion in 1989 (*Webster v. Reproductive Health Services*). It was clear that four justices, including Scalia, were anxious to overturn the previous cases supporting abortion, but they could not take action unless Justice O'Connor indicated that she was ready to provide the needed fifth vote. In the controversial *Webster* case approving Missouri's restrictions on abortions in public hospitals, three of the justices (Rehnquist, White, and Kennedy) diplomatically accommodated Justice O'Connor by claiming to agree with her that they had not yet been confronted with an appropriate case for reexamining *Roe v. Wade*. Rather than join his colleagues in patiently cultivating O'Connor's uncertain support, Scalia attacked O'Connor *and* his three allies for not forthrightly reversing *Roe*. If O'Connor is truly unsure of her fundamental views about the constitutionality of abortion, will she be inclined to join a coalition with a justice who condemns her?

Interpersonal relationships between justices not only have potential consequences for the outcomes of specific cases, they may also affect the institution of the Court when harsh personal criticisms are expressed publicly in judicial opinions. As Stuart Taylor observes:

> But there is still a serious cost to public brawling on the bench: The more the justices question each other's basic common sense and good faith, the more they may deplete the reservoir of popular good will that is so essential to their

---

4. Antonin Scalia, "The Disease as Cure," *Washington University Law Quarterly* (1979): 147.
   5. Ibid., p. 148.

singular role in American life. They might eventually find their rulings dismissed as the work of unelected, unprincipled politicians.

That would be a shame, because public respect for the [C]ourt—based partly on ignorance and partly on myth—is fundamentally well-placed.[6]

Although the Supreme Court is a political institution and the development of constitutional law is the product of politics, the justices struggle to fulfill constitutional values, as they see them, and they are less inclined than other political actors to make decisions based upon naked self-interest. Moreover, because of the public's belief in the Supreme Court as a "legal" institution and other political institutions' acquiescence to the legitimacy of Court decisions, the Supreme Court has often been a stabilizing force within a conflict-laden society.

JOHNSON v. TRANSPORTATION AGENCY, SANTA CLARA COUNTY

480 U.S. 616 (1987)

[Justices BRENNAN, MARSHALL, BLACKMUN, POWELL, STEVENS, and O'CONNOR determined that an employer could take an applicant's gender into consideration under an affirmative action plan when making promotion decisions for a position in which women had traditionally been underrepresented. The case concerned interpretation of Title VII, the employment discrimination statute, rather than the Constitution].

Justice SCALIA dissenting [joined by Chief Justice REHNQUIST. Justice WHITE also dissented]:

. . . A statute designed to establish a color-blind and gender-blind workplace has thus been converted into a powerful engine of racism and sexism, not merely *permitting* intentional race- and sex-based discrimination, but often making it through operation of the legal system, practically compelled.

. . . [T]he only losers in the process are the Johnsons of the country, for whom Title VII has been not merely repealed but actually inverted. The irony is that these individuals—predominantly unknown, unaffluent, unorganized—suffer this injustice at the hands of a Court fond of thinking itself the champion of the politically impotent. I dissent.

---

6. Taylor, p. A11.

WARDS COVE PACKING CO. v. ATONIO

109 S. Ct. 2115 (1989)

[Chief Justice REHNQUIST, Justices WHITE, O'CONNOR, SCALIA, and KENNEDY decided that plaintiffs suing under Title VII for employment discrimination can no longer rely solely upon statistics to show that employers' practices have a discriminatory impact. Contrary to a 1971 precedent, plaintiffs must now identify specific discriminatory employment practices].

Justice BLACKMUN dissenting [joined by Justices BRENNAN and MARSHALL. Justice STEVENS also dissented]:

. . . Today a bare majority of the Court takes three major strides backwards in the battle against race discrimination. It reaches out to make last Term's plurality opinion in *Watson v. Fort Worth Bank & Trust* . . . the law, thereby upsetting the longstanding distribution of burdens of proof in Title VII disparate-impact cases. It bars the use of internal workforce comparisons in the making of a prima facie case of discrimination, even where the structure of the industry in question renders any other statistical comparison meaningless. And it requires practice-by-practice statistical proof of causation, even where, as here, such proof would be impossible.

The harshness of these results is well demonstrated by the facts of this case. The salmon industry as described by this record takes us back to a kind of overt and institutionalized discrimination we have not dealt with in years: a total residential and work environment organized on principles of racial stratification and segregation, which, as Justice Stevens points out, resembles a plantation economy. . . . This industry long has been characterized by a taste for discrimination of the old-fashioned sort: a preference for hiring nonwhites to fill its lowest-level positions, on the condition that they stay there. The majority's legal rulings essentially immunize these practices from attack under a Title VII disparate-impact analysis.

Sadly, this comes as no surprise. One wonders whether the majority still believes that race discrimination—or, more accurately, race discrimination against nonwhites—is a problem in our society, or even remembers that it ever was. . . .

WEBSTER v. REPRODUCTIVE HEALTH SERVICES

109 S. Ct. 3040 (1989)

[While claiming to keep *Roe v. Wade* intact, Chief Justice REHNQUIST, Justices WHITE, O'CONNOR, and KENNEDY upheld a Missouri statute prohibiting abortions in public hospitals and declaring that life begins at conception. In his concurring opinion, Justice SCALIA criticized his colleagues in the majority for not forthrightly overturning previous decisions supporting a woman's constitutional right of choice regarding abortion].

Justice SCALIA concurring:

. . . .

The outcome of today's case will doubtless be heralded as a triumph of judicial statesmanship. It is not that, unless it is statesmanlike needlessly to prolong this Court's self-awarded sovereignty over a field where it has little proper business since the answers to most of the cruel questions posed are political and not juridical—a sovereignty which therefore quite properly, but to the great damage of the Court, makes it the object of the sort of organized public pressure that political institutions in a democracy ought to receive.

Justice O'CONNOR's assertion... that a " 'fundamental rule of judicial restraint' " requires us to avoid reconsidering *Roe* [*v. Wade*], cannot be taken seriously. By finessing *Roe* we do not, as she suggests, ... adhere to the strict and venerable rule that we should avoid " 'decid[ing] questions of a constitutional nature.' " ... What is involved, therefore, is not the rule of avoiding constitutional issues where possible, but the quite separate principle that we will not " 'formulate a rule of constitutional law broader than is required by the precise facts to which it is applied.' " The latter is a sound general principle, but one often departed from when good reason exists. Just this Term, for example, in an opinion authored by Justice O'CONNOR [we departed from the principle she is asserting here]. . . . Also this Term, in an opinion joined by Justice O'CONNOR [we similarly departed from the principle she asserts]. . . .

The real question, then, is whether there are valid reasons to go beyond the most stingy possible holding today. It seems to me there are not only valid but compelling ones. Ordinarily, speaking no more broadly than is absolutely required avoids throwing settled law into confusion; doing so today preserves a chaos that is evident to anyone who can read and count. Alone sufficient to justify a broad holding is the fact that our retaining control, through *Roe*, of what I believe to be, a political issue, continuously distorts the public perception of the role of this Court. We can now look forward to at least another Term with carts full of mail from the public, and streets full of demonstrators, urging us—their unelected and life-tenured judges who have been awarded these extraordinary undemocratic characteristics precisely in order that we might follow the law despite the popular will—to follow the popular will. Indeed, I expect we can look forward to even more of that than before, given our indecisive decision today. . . .

. . . Given the Court's newly contracted abstemiousness, what will it take, one must wonder, to permit us to reach that fundamental question? The result of our vote today is that we will not reconsider that prior opinion [in *Roe v. Wade*], even if most of the Justices think it is wrong, unless we have before us a statute that in fact contradicts it—and even then (under our newly discovered "no-broader-than-necessary" requirement) only minor problematical aspects of *Roe* will be reconsidered, unless one expects State legislatures to adopt provisions whose compliance with *Roe* cannot even be argued with a straight face. It thus appears that the mansion of constitutionalized abortion-law, constructed overnight in *Roe v. Wade*, must be disassembled door-jamb by door-jamb, and never entirely brought down, no matter how wrong it may be.

Of the four courses we might have chosen today—to reaffirm *Roe*, to overrule it explicitly, to overrule it *sub silentio*, or to avoid the question—the last is the least responsible. . . . I concur in the judgment of the Court and strongly dissent from the manner in which it has been reached.

COUNTY OF ALLEGHENY v. AMERICAN CIVIL LIBERTIES UNION

109 S. Ct. 3086 (1989)

[Justices BRENNAN, BLACKMUN, MARSHALL, STEVENS, and O'CONNOR decided that the First Amendment Establishment Clause had been violated by the prominent display of a nativity scene alone in a county courthouse without a Christmas tree, Santa Claus, or other non-religious symbols of the holiday season].

Justice BLACKMUN delivered the opinion of the Court [joined for Part V by Justices BRENNAN, MARSHALL, STEVENS, and O'CONNOR]:

. . . .

V

. . . .

Justice KENNEDY's reasons for permitting the creche on the Grand Staircase [of the county courthouse] and his condemnation of the

Court's reasons for deciding otherwise are so far-reaching in their implication that they require a response in some depth:

. . . .

. . . Thus, *Marsh* [*v. Chambers*, 1984, approving the constitutionality of prayers at legislative sessions,] plainly does not stand for the sweeping proposition Justice KENNEDY apparently would ascribe to it, namely, that all accepted practices 200 years old and their equivalents are constitutional today. . . . Although Justice KENNEDY said that he "cannot comprehend" how the creche display could be invalid after *Marsh*, . . . surely he is able to distinguish between a specifically Christian symbol, like a creche, and more general religious references, like the legislative prayers in *Marsh*.

Justice KENNEDY's reading of *Marsh* would gut the core of the Establishment Clause, as this Court understands it. . . .

. . . Justice KENNEDY's misreading of *Marsh* is predicated on a failure to recognize the bedrock Establishment Clause principle that, regardless of history, government may not demonstrate a preference for a particular faith. . . .

. . . [Justice KENNEDY] also suggests that [as a result of our decision] a city would demonstrate an unconstitutional preference for Christianity if it displayed a Christian symbol during every major Christian holiday but did not display the religious symbols of other faiths during other religious holidays. . . . But, for Justice KENNEDY, would it be enough of a preference for Christianity if that city each year displayed a creche for 40 days during the Christmas season and a cross for 40 days during Lent (and never the symbols of other religions)? If so, then what if there were no cross but the 40-day creche display contained a sign exhorting the city's citizens "to offer up their devotions to God their Creator, and his Son Jesus Christ, the Redeemer of the World"? . . .

The point of these rhetorical questions is obvious. In order to define precisely what government could and could not do under Justice KENNEDY's "proselytization" test, the Court would have to decide a series of cases with particular fact patterns that fall along the spectrum of government references to religion. . . . If one wished to be "uncharitable" to Justice KENNEDY [quoting from Justice KENNEDY's reference to BLACKMUN's opinion], one could say that his methodology requires counting the number of days during which the government displays Christian symbols and subtracting from this the number of days during which non-Christian symbols are displayed, divided by the number of different non-Christian religions represented in the displays, and then somehow factoring into this equation the prominence of the display's location and the degree to which each symbol possesses an inherently proselytizing quality. . . . Justice KENNEDY should be wary of accusing the Court's formulation as "using little more than intuition and a tape measure," . . . lest he find his own formulation convicted of an identical charge. . . .

Although Justice KENNEDY repeatedly accuses the Court of harboring a "latent hostility" or "callous indifference" toward religion, . . . nothing could be further from the truth, and the accusations could be said to be as offensive as they are absurd. Justice KENNEDY apparently has misperceived a respect for religious pluralism, a respect commanded by the Constitution, as hostility or indifference to religion. No misperception could be more antithetical to the values embodied in the Establishment Clause.

Justice KENNEDY's accusations are shot from a weapon triggered by [a] proposition . . . [that] is flawed at its foundation. . . .

Justice KENNEDY dissenting [joined by Chief Justice REHNQUIST, Justices WHITE and SCALIA]:

. . . [The majority's] view of the Establishment Clause reflects an unjustified hostility toward religion, a hostility inconsistent with our history and our precedents. . . .

III

. . . .

In addition to disregarding precedents and historical fact, the majority's approach to government use of religious symbolism threatens to trivialize constitutional adjudication. By mischaracterizing the Court's opinion in *Lynch* [*v. Donnelly*, 1984, approving a city-owned nativity display along with Santa Claus, reindeer, and other nonreligious Christmas symbols] as an endorsement-in-context test, . . . the majority embraces a jurisprudence of minutiae. . . .

My description of the majority's test, though perhaps uncharitable, is intended to illustrate the inevitable difficulties with its application. This test could provide workable guidance to the lower courts, if ever, only after this Court has decided a long series of holiday display cases, using little more than intuition and a tape measure. Deciding cases on the basis of such an unguided examination of marginalia is irreconcilable with the imperative of applying neutral principles in constitutional adjudication. "It would be appalling to conduct litigation under the Establishment Clause as if it were a trademark case, with experts testifying about whether one display is really like another, and witnesses testifying they were offended—but would have been less so were the creche five feet closer to a jumbo candy cane." ...

... If there be such a person as the "reasonable observer," I am quite certain that he or she will take away a salient message from our holding in this case: the Supreme Court of the United States has concluded that the First Amendment creates classes of religions based on the relative numbers of their adherents. Those religions enjoying the largest following must be consigned to the status of least-favored faiths so as to avoid any possible risk of offending members of minority religions. ...

V

The approach adopted by the majority contradicts important values embodied in the [Establishment] Clause. Obsessive, implacable resistance to all but the most carefully scripted and secularized forms of accommodation requires this Court to act as a censor, issuing national decrees as to what is orthodox and what is not. What is orthodox, in this context, means what is secular; the only Christmas the State can acknowledge is one in which references to religion have been held to a minimum. The Court thus lends its assistance to an Orwellian rewriting of history as many understand it. I can conceive of no judicial function more antithetical to the First Amendment. ...

HOLLAND v. ILLINOIS

110 S. Ct. 803 (1990)

[Chief Justice REHNQUIST, Justices SCALIA, O'CONNOR, WHITE, and KENNEDY rejected a white defendant's claim that the prosecution's use of peremptory challenges to exclude African-American jurors violated the Sixth Amendment's requirement of a "fair cross section" represented in juries].

Justice SCALIA delivered the opinion of the Court [joined by Chief Justice REHNQUIST, Justices WHITE, O'CONNOR, and KENNEDY]:

. . . .

III

. . . .

Justice MARSHALL's dissent rolls out the ultimate weapon, the accusation of insensitivity to racial discrimination—which will lose its intimidating effect if it continues to be fired so randomly. . . . His Sixth Amendment claim would be just as strong if the object of exclusion had been, not blacks, but postmen, or lawyers, or clergymen, or any number of other identifiable groups. Race as such has nothing to do with the legal issue in this case.

. . . [I]t is no more reasonable to portray this as a civil rights case than it is to characterize a proposal for increased murder penalties as an anti-discrimination law. . . .

Justice MARSHALL dissenting [joined by Justices BRENNAN and BLACKMUN. Justice STEVENS also dissented]:

The Court decides today that a prosecutor's racially motivated exclusion of Afro-Americans from the petit jury does not violate the fair cross-section requirement of the Sixth Amendment. To reach this startling result, the majority misrepresents the values underlying the fair cross-section requirement, overstates the difficulties associated with the elimination of racial discrimination in jury selection, and ignores the clear import of well-grounded precedents. . . .

II

. . . .

The fundamental premise underlying the majority's analysis in this case is the assertion that the sole purpose of the Sixth Amendment's jury trial requirement is to secure for the defendant an impartial jury. The majority defends this thesis by constructing a false dichotomy: the fair cross-section requirement *either* protects impartiality *or* guarantees a petit jury that mirrors the community from which it is drawn. From these two options, the majority selects impartiality as its governing principle. . . . The remainder of its analysis proceeds from and is dependent upon the assumption that impartiality is the sole end of the fair cross-section requirement. That assumption is flatly false, and the conclusion to which it leads is one that I cannot imagine that even the majority would accept in all its implications. . . .

If the majority's selective amnesia with respect to our cases in this area is surprising, its suggestion that recognition of petitioner's Sixth Amendment claim "would cripple the device of peremptory challenge," . . . can only be described as staggering. . . .

III

The majority today insulates an especially invidious form of racial discrimination in the selection of petit juries from Sixth Amendment scrutiny. To reach this result, the majority chooses to pretend that it writes on a blank slate, ignoring precedent after precedent. . . .

Even had the majority marshaled the sorts of arguments that normally accompany the rejection of the principles underlying a whole line of cases, I would remain dubious. The elimination of racial discrimination in our system of criminal justice is not a constitutional goal that should be lightly set aside. Because the majority apparently disagrees, I dissent.[2]

Questions

1. In *Johnson*, note Justice Scalia's use of sarcasm in saying that the Court is "fond of thinking itself the champion of the politically impotent." Why did he not say "a Court that *used to be* the champions of the powerless"? Is Scalia implying that the Supreme Court is self-deluded to think that it was ever the protector of the politically powerless? How should holdovers from the Warren era, such as Justices Brennan and Marshall, feel about such a statement?
2. In contemporary American society, educated people generally attempt to show that they are sensitive to the problems of racial prejudice even if they disagree with specific remedial public policies such as affirmative action and school desegregation. How might Justice Blackmun's criticism in *Wards Cove* affect members of the majority? Will it encourage them to reconsider their position? Will they decide that such comments from Blackmun cannot be taken seriously? Will they defend themselves in future cases against the serious charge of insensitivity to racial discrimination?
3. In *Webster*, why is Justice Scalia so concerned about organized political pressure directed at the Supreme Court? If it has no effect on the justices' decisions (as the justices would undoubtedly claim), why should he care about carts full of mail or demonstrators outside the building?
4. How will the other members of the majority in *Webster* feel about Scalia's sarcastic criticism of their lack of "judicial statesmanship"?

2. The majority considers "random[]" my suggestion that its opinion today signals a retreat from our previous efforts to eradicate racial discrimination. . . . Our cases have repeatedly used the Sixth Amendment's fair cross-section requirement as a weapon to combat racial discrimination. . . . Yet today, the majority says that the Sixth Amendment is no more concerned with discrimination against Afro-Americans than it is with discrimination against "postmen." . . . The majority concludes that "[r]ace as such has nothing to do with the legal issue in this case." . . . I read these statements as a retreat; that the majority has so little understanding of our Sixth Amendment jurisprudence that it considers that criticism "random[]" is, if anything, proof that it is right on the mark [to label this a retreat].

5. If Scalia and the other three justices are trying to persuade Justice O'Connor to provide the fifth vote to overturn *Roe v. Wade*, how will their efforts be affected by Scalia's comment that O'Connor's opinion "cannot be taken seriously"? What about his efforts to point out O'Connor's inconsistencies with her previous decisions? Is she likely to be persuaded by these tactics? Might she defend herself by resisting any inclination to join Scalia's position?

6. In *County of Allegheny*, note how Justice Blackmun mimics the criticisms contained in Justice Kennedy's dissenting opinion. They both apply "uncharitable" analyses of the other's proposed test and they both declare that the other's conclusions are "antithetical" to the First Amendment. How should Kennedy expect Blackmun (and the others in the majority) to react when he labels their legal test as "using little other than intuition and a tape measure"? How should the majority react to Kennedy's claim that they have engaged in "an Orwellian rewriting of history"? Is Kennedy making any effort to persuade his colleagues by deriding their views? Are dissenting opinions actually written for different purposes (and for different audiences)?

7. When Blackmun labels Kennedy's "accusation" as "offensive as well as absurd," is he admitting that Kennedy's opinion has made him angry? How might this affect his willingness to listen to Kennedy's views in other cases?

8. In *Holland*, once again Scalia employs sarcasm by graphically alluding to Justice Marshall "roll[ing] out the ultimate weapon." When Scalia says such accusations "will lose their intimidating effect," is he implying that the assertion of racial discrimination claims has improperly influenced previous decisions by intimidating justices who feared being labeled as 'racists'?

9. When Scalia says the accusations "continue[] to be fired . . . randomly," is he implying that justices raise the issue of racial discrimination too frequently and in inappropriate cases?

10. Among members of the Supreme Court, Justice Marshall's life experiences gave him unique exposure to the problems of racial discrimination. Prior to his retirement in 1991, he was the only justice to grow up as a victimized minority group member in a segregated Southern border state (Maryland); the only justice to be dragged from his car at night toward a tree with a noose by a lynch mob composed of Tennessee police officers; the only justice to travel throughout the segregated South representing victims in race discrimination cases; and the only justice who, along with his family, faces the subtle (and not-so-subtle) problems of racial prejudice that continue to exist in American society. Given the uniqueness of Justice Marshall's experience, should Justice Scalia give more serious consideration to Marshall's claim before flatly and sarcastically rejecting it? Should Justice Scalia defer to Justice Marshall's broader experience and knowledge about issues of racial discrimination?

11. Does Scalia's opinion represent an aggressive counterattack against opinions, such as Blackmun's in *Ward Cove*, which allege that the emerging conservative majority is insensitive to the issue of racial discrimination against minority groups?

12. Will members of the majority in *Holland* be less inclined to listen to Justice Marshall's views when Marshall accuses them of such things as "selective amnesia"?
13. Does the tone of Scalia's opinion indicate that, in the deeply divided Supreme Court, members of the emerging majority have already stopped listening to Justice Marshall and the dissenters on discrimination issues? If so, have the Supreme Court's collegial decision-making processes deteriorated?

Index of Cases

(Boldface denotes case excerpts.)

Adamson v. California, 332 U.S. 46 (1947), **83–86**, 87, 90, 91

Arizona v. Roberson, 486 U.S. 675 (1988), 120–23, 126

Barefoot v. Estelle, 463 U.S. 880 (1983), 117

Barron v. Baltimore, 32 U.S. 243 (1833), 80, 85

Berk v. Laird, 429 F.2d 302 (2d Cir. 1970), 47

Boos v. Barry, 485 U.S. 312 (1988), 147

Bounds v. Smith, 430 U.S. 817 (1977), 116

Bowsher v. Synar, 478 U.S. 714 (1986), **13–21**, 24, 36–37

Bradley v. Fisher, 13 Wall. 335 (1872), 51

Bradwell v. Illinois, 16 Wall. 130 (1873), 65

Brown v. Board of Education, 347 U.S. 483 (1954), 5, 62, 66–67, 77–78

Buckley v. Valeo, 424 U.S. 1 (1976), 22

Butler v. McKellar, 110 S. Ct. 1212 (1990), 96, **120–24**, 126

Chaplinsky v. New Hampshire, 315 U.S. 568 (1942), 137, 141

Chicago, Burlington & Quincy Railroad v. Chicago, 166 U.S. 226 (1897), 81, 92

City of Akron v. Akron Center for Reproductive Health, 462 U.S. 416 (1983), 130

Civil Rights Cases, 109 U.S. 3 (1883), 66–68, 77

Coker v. Georgia, 433 U.S. 584 (1977), 97

County of Allegheny v. American Civil Liberties Union, 109 S. Ct. 3086 (1988), **161–64**, 167

Daniel v. Paul, 395 U.S. 298 (1969), 74–77, 78

Duncan v. Louisiana, 391 U.S. 145 (1968), **88–91**, 92

Enmund v. Florida, 458 U.S. 782 (1982), 95, **96–98**, 99, 101–4, 124–25, 155

Edwards v. Arizona, 451 U.S. 477 (1981), 121–23

Fuentes v. Shevin, 407 U.S. 67 (1972), 4

Furman v. Georgia, 408 U.S. 238
(1972), 95, 113

Gitlow v. New York, 268 U.S. 652
(1925), 81, 91–92
Gregg v. Georgia, 428 U.S. 153
(1976), 95, 114

Harris v. McRae, 448 U.S. 297
(1980), 130
Heart of Atlanta Motel v. United
States, 379 U.S. 241 (1964),
72–74, 78
Holland v. Illinois, 110 S. Ct. 803
(1990), 164–66, 167–68
Holtzman v. Schlesinger, 414 U.S.
1304 and 414 U.S. 1316 (1973),
44–46, 47–48, 62
Humphrey's Executor v. United
States, 295 U.S. 602 (1935),
15–16, 24, 35

Immigration and Naturalization
Service v. Chadha, 462 U.S.
919 (1983), 12, 15–19

Johnson v. Transportation Agency,
Santa Clara County, 480 U.S.
616 (1987), 158, 167

Katzenbach v. McClung, 379 U.S.
294 (1964), 71–74, 78
Korematsu v. United States, 323
U.S. 214 (1944), 66

Lemon v. Kurtzman, 403 U.S. 602
(1971), 156
Lochner v. New York, 198 U.S. 45
(1905), 65
Lynch v. Donnelly, 465 U.S. 668
(1984), 163

McCleskey v. Kemp, 481 U.S. 278
(1987), 96, 107–16, 125–26
McCleskey v. Zant, 111 S. Ct. 1454
(1991), 95
Maher v. Roe, 432 U.S. 464 (1977),
130

Marbury v. Madison, 5 U.S. 137
(1803), 10
Marsh v. Chambers, 463 U.S. 783
(1983), 156, 162
Miranda v. Arizona, 384 U.S. 436
(1966), 93, 121, 123
Missouri v. Jenkins, 110 S. Ct. 1651
(1990), 42, 57–62, 63, 66
Mistretta v. United States, 109 S.
Ct. 647 (1989), 13, 28–36, 37
Mitchell v. W. T. Grant Co., 416
U.S. 600 (1974), 4
Mitchell v. United States, 386 U.S.
972 (1967), 43
Mora v. McNamara, 389 U.S. 934
(1967), 43–44, 62
Morrison v. Olson, 108 S. Ct. 2597
(1988), 13, 21–27, 36–37
Murray v. Giarratano, 109 S. Ct.
2765 (1989), 96, 116–20, 126
Myers v. United States, 272 U.S. 52
(1926), 15–16, 24

New York v. Quarles, 467 U.S. 649
(1984), 93

Palko v. Connecticut, 302 U.S. 319
(1937), 81–83, 84–85, 87, 89,
90–92
Pennsylvania v. Finley, 481 U.S. 551
(1987), 116–17, 119
Penry v. Lynaugh, 109 S. Ct. 2934
(1989), 121
Plessy v. Ferguson, 163 U.S. 537
(1896), 65, 77
Powell v. Alabama, 287 U.S. 45
(1932), 119
Prize Cases, 67 U.S. 935 (1863), 47

Regents of the University of
California v. Bakke, 438 U.S.
265 (1978), 157
Rochin v. California, 342 U.S. 165
(1952), 86–88, 91
Roe v. Wade, 410 U.S. 113 (1973),
129–30, 157, 159, 160–61, 167

Ross v. Moffitt, 417 U.S. 600 (1974), 116–17

Schlesinger v. Holtzman, 414 U.S. 1321 (1973), 48–49
Smith v. Goguen, 415 U.S. 566 (1974), 146, 152
Snyder v. Massachusetts, 291 U.S. 97 (1934), 90
Spallone v. United States, 110 S. Ct. 625 (1990), 42, 52–57, 63
Street v. New York, 394 U.S. 576 (1969), 134–39, 152
Stump v. Sparkman, 435 U.S. 349 (1978), 42, 49–52, 63
Synar v. U.S., 626 F.Supp. 1374 (D.D.C. 1986), 14

Teague v. Lane, 109 S. Ct. 1060 (1989), 122
Texas v. Johnson, 109 S. Ct. 2533 (1989), 131, 139–45, 146–52
Thornburgh v. American College of Obstetricians and Gynecologists, 476 U.S. 747 (1986), 130
Tison v. Arizona, 481 U.S. 137 (1987), 95, 99–107, 124–25, 155

United States v. Eichman, 110 S. Ct. 2404 (1990), 131, 147–52, 153
United States v. Germaine, 99 U.S. 508 (1879), 22
United States v. Nixon, 418 U.S. 683 (1974), 5, 9, 11
United States v. O'Brien, 391 U.S. 367 (1968), 132–34, 147
United Steelworkers of America v. Weber, 443 U.S. 193 (1979), 156

Wards Cove Packing Co. v. Atonio, 109 S. Ct. 2115 (1989), 159, 167–68
Watson v. Fort Worth Bank and Trust, 487 U.S. 977 (1988), 159
Webster v. Reproductive Health Services, 109 S. Ct. 3040 (1989), 130, 157, 159–61, 167
Wickard v. Filburn, 317 U.S. 111 (1942), 69, 72

Youngstown Sheet and Tube Co. v. Sawyer, 343 U.S. 579 (1952), 15, 32–33, 37, 47